PREACHING AND WORSHIP

Preaching and Its Partners
A series edited by Paul Scott Wilson

PREACHING AND PRACTICAL MINISTRY
Ronald J. Allen

PREACHING AND WORSHIP
Thomas H. Troeger

\

PREACHING AND WORSHIP

THOMAS H. TROEGER

CHALICE
PRESS

ST. LOUIS, MISSOURI

All scripture quotations, unless otherwise indicated, are from the *New Revised Standard Version Bible*, copyright 1989, Division of Christian Education of the National Council of the Churches of Christ in the United States of America. Used by permission. All rights reserved.

Scripture quotations marked (NEB) are from the *New English Bible*, copyright Oxford University Press and Cambridge University Press 1961, 1970. Reprinted by permission.

Cover design: Michael A. Domínguez
Cover art: © 1998 Artville
Interior design: Wynn Younker
Art direction: Michael A. Domínguez

This book is printed on acid-free, recycled paper.

Visit Chalice Press on the World Wide Web at
www.chalicepress.com

10 9 8 7 6 5 4 3 2 1   03 04 05 06 07 08

Library of Congress Cataloging–in–Publication Data

Troeger, Thomas H., 1945-
  Preaching and worship / by Thomas H. Troeger.– 1st ed.
    p. cm. – (Preaching and its partners)
Includes bibliographical references.
  ISBN 0-8272-2978-X (alk. paper)
  1. Christianity and culture. 2. Preaching. 3. Worship. I. Title. II. Series.
  BR115.C8T76 2003
  251–dc21
                                                              2003011293

Printed in the United States of America

For
K. D.,
extraordinary student assistant
pastor of many gifts
a bright and shining soul

CONTENTS

ACKNOWLEDGMENTS

I am indebted to Professor Paul Scott Wilson, who invited me to write this volume in the Chalice series *Preaching and Its Partners.*

I also want to thank Virginia Theological Seminary, which invited me to give the Sprigg Lectures in October 2001. There I was able to try out many of the ideas that I have now revised for this book.

A special word of gratitude is due to the Reverend Kimberly Dickerson, who was one of the most gifted Master of Divinity students I have taught. She was my student assistant when I began this work. Both her research and her conversation were helpful in clarifying a number of issues that I address.

I also want to thank Sally Bowersox, who became my assistant near the end of the project. She traced down a number of essential details.

Finally, I acknowledge Iliff School of Theology, the intellectually stimulating and diverse community in which I learn new things day by day about the interrelationship of worship, culture, and preaching.

1

Culture as a Constellation of the Senses

Parable in a Noodle Shop

I begin in a noodle shop, which might seem a strange place to start a book about the interrelationship of preaching, worship, and culture. But let me tell you about eating a particular bowl of noodles, and you will soon see that it has great deal to do with the topic.

The noodle shop was in Kyoto, Japan, where I was the guest of three professors who had asked what Japanese food I most enjoy.

"*Soba* [noodles]," I said, "the long brown ones you serve with fish broth and pieces of *tempura* [deep fried seafood and vegetables]."

The three professors took me to their favorite noodle shop, and all four of us ordered noodles. Their bowls came with chopsticks and mine with a fork, spoon, and knife, a gesture of hospitality by my hosts. They bowed over the table, lifted the bowls to their chins, and began using a rapid circular motion with their chopsticks to shove the contents into their mouths with a sucking sound. I slowly twirled a few noodles around my fork while pointing the tines into my spoon. Then I silently placed the small bundle of noodles in my mouth.

After several of these motions, I noticed that my friends had stopped eating and were watching me closely.

"You don't like your *soba*?" one of them asked.

"Oh, the noodles are delicious," I replied.

"But you make no sound!" two of them exclaimed in unison.

"My parents taught me never to make a sound while eating noodles," I explained.

My Japanese friends found this instruction incomprehensible. They asked me to continue eating. They wanted to see me twirl my noodles again and put them soundlessly in my mouth. Then they laughed, and I, too, laughed at the utterly different ways we had been taught to eat noodles.

One of my friends suggested, "Why don't you try to make some sound with your noodles to let the proprietor know that you are enjoying your *soba*."

I sucked the dangling ends of a few noodles through my mouth, making a faint slurping sound. I continued to do this for about a minute, then realized that I had returned to my usual silent noodle consumption. My upbringing overrode my best intention to demonstrate audible delight in my noodles.

The culture in which we are raised indelibly marks us: "It is no exaggeration to say that from the very onset of life the emergent human being is being catechized into a cosmology—a sense of the way the universe runs and his or her place in the scheme of things."[1] Note that word *catechized*. It is well chosen because catechesis is the technical term for the teaching of the church, and there is a religious quality to the behaviors that any culture insists on. If we violate those behaviors, we feel we have broken a sacred taboo. My Japanese friends were catechized to slurp their noodles; I was catechized to make no sound.

Childhood training was more powerful than any adult desire to oblige my hosts. Although I might say rationally to myself, "It is all right, Tom, to make sound with your noodles," I was dealing with something that reaches deeper than reason. The rituals of eating that my parents had taught me from childhood were controlling my behavior. They were second nature to me, a part of my being that I had absorbed so completely that they guided me like an automatic pilot.

My Japanese friends and I settled into a deep discussion about theology and the church. But turning from table manners to words did not end the cultural contrasts, even though all of my friends spoke English. Just as our ways of eating noodles differed, so did our strategies of verbal communication. Their way of disagreeing was disarming: They nodded yes to everything I said, even when they believed the opposite. Staying in contact was more important to them than settling an issue. My Japanese friends never displayed the American penchant for trying to argue the other person into accepting one's point of view. Their communication was more indirect, and their vocal inflection, which featured less dramatic changes in dynamic level than American speech, increased the sense of different verbal strategies.

The work of Eunjoo Kim later helped me understand the differences I had experienced in the noodle shop:

> East Asian culture, influenced by Confucian and Buddhist spirituality, respects harmonious relations. Harmony and unity are more valued than difference and conflict. In this accommodation-oriented culture, the goal of communication is to seek agreement or consensus rather than disagreement or division. As a way of arriving at consensus, the speaker appeals to the heart of the audience. That is, rather than stressing points through a manipulative or coercive manner, which may clash with those of others, Asian persuasion seeks the audience's voluntary consensus with the speaker by guiding them to feel as the speaker feels, to see from the same perspective, and finally to be awakened intuitively as the speaker was.[2]

The Element in Which We Swim

Eating noodles and conversing with my Japanese friends, I remembered a former colleague who taught theology and whose doctorate was in cultural anthropology. One of her favorite statements was, "Culture is to human beings as water is to fish."[3] We swim in it. It is the element in which we live, the worldview that shapes who we are and how we act. As long as my Japanese friends ate only among themselves and as long as I ate only with people raised in the same culture as myself, we would be far less aware of the peculiar character of our practices. We would be "swimming" in them.

Anthropologists have attempted to refine the definition of "culture" so that it can be used with more precision. Here, for example, is a definition of culture by a scholar writing in the last third of the nineteenth century: Culture, "taken in its wide ethnographic sense, is that complex whole which includes knowledge, belief, art, morals, law, custom, and any other capabilities and habits acquired by man

[*sic*] as a member of society."[4] This definition is characteristic of
Victorian anthropologists who wrote about culture as the rational
creation of human minds responding to needs.

Franz Boas, an influential anthropologist of the early twentieth
century, helped us to see that "however rational and sensible our
beliefs and practices may be...we have an emotional attachment
to them, so that an important accompaniment of all learning is a
strong devotion to the patterns that are acquired." Boas made
this point by saying that "cultural beliefs and practices have
emotional association, in that deviations become intolerable to
the members of society."[5]

These early efforts at definition suggested that culture was a
relatively stable element of human life. But scholars writing at the
start of the third millennium have begun to stress the dynamic nature
of culture:

> In contrast to earlier notions of culture as the deposit or ac-
> cumulation of knowledge or meaning produced by elites, or
> as a body of beliefs and values shared by all members of a
> group such as a nation or religious community, culture now
> is viewed as the dynamic and contentious process by which
> meaning, and with it power, is produced, circulated, and ne-
> gotiated by all who reside within a particular cultural
> milieu...Culture is the process by which meaning is pro-
> duced, contended for, and continually renegotiated and the
> context in which individual and communal identities are
> mediated into being.[6]

A Culture Is Defined by Its Sensorium

Although cultures are dynamic social realties, they also have
distinctive characteristics. My Japanese friends and I were keenly
aware of our differences as they slurped and I silently ate my noodles.
When we encounter another culture, we discover that actions that
we assumed to be the "natural way of doing things" are in reality
learned behavior, something taught us by our culture. For the
anthropologist, "culture is all learned behavior which is socially
acquired, that is, the material and nonmaterial traits which are passed
on from one generation to another. They are both transmittable and
accumulative, and they are cultural in the sense that they are
transmitted by the society, not by genes."[7]

Our home culture has given us answers to questions that are
implicit in the traditions and practices of all cultures:

- How will we use our eyes?
- How will we use our ears?
- How will we use our bodies?
- How will we use language?
- What is the meaning of how we use eyes, ears, bodies, and language?

The answers to these questions vary so tremendously that

> it is useful to think of cultures in terms of the organization of the sensorium. By the sensorium we mean here the entire sensory apparatus as an operational complex. The difference in cultures…can be thought of as differences in the sensorium, the organization of which is in part determined by culture while at the same time it makes culture…Man's [*sic*] sensory perceptions are abundant and overwhelming. He cannot attend to them all at once. In great part a given culture teaches him one or another way of productive specialization. It brings him to organize his sensorium by attending to some types of perception more than others, by making an issue of certain ones.[8]

The sensorium of a church at worship is deeply rooted and difficult to change. Consider, for example, a single sense: smell. There are churches that use incense so heavily that its fragrance hangs in the air even when no service is in progress, and there are churches that have never considered engaging the sense of smell in worship.

If a pastor were to eliminate incense from the one church or introduce it in the other, there would likely be a revolt in the congregation. The people would feel that the sensorium of the church had been violated.

I do not know if there is any such thing as a neutral smell. I assume that certain smells are nauseous to all human beings: for example, decaying flesh and rotten fruit. But I could be wrong about this, and I know for certain there are smells I enjoy that others find abhorrent. I like the smell of hamburger on an open grill, but I have vegetarian friends who grow sick at the odor. The important principle is that how we use our nose, along with all our other senses, is a function of something greater than our physiological nature. We learn from our culture what is acceptable and unacceptable to each sense.

Even a change that keeps within the boundaries of the sensorium may meet resistance because it violates the expectation that worship will provide a familiar path to the holy. Consider, for example, how difficult it is to change the way a church serves communion. Although clergy often jest about church members who say, "We never did it that way before," the resistance to change flows from the nature of ritual as an action "repeated in regular and predictable ways, both in religious and secular contexts, serving so many purposes that summary is impossible."[9]

One partial way to define culture is to say it is the constellation of ritual behaviors by which adults conduct their lives and which they pass on to their children.

- "Say, 'thank you.'"
- "Shake hands."
- "Shut your eyes and bow your head when we pray."

More important than our words are our actions, which children observe, imitate, and master by doing. They learn from us the pattern of our sensorium. They see and hear that the use of the body and the voice varies as we move from intimate family settings to public gatherings.

> Postures and gestures are learnt principally by imitation and soon become "natural" and unreflective. All bodily practices, such as talking, walking, reading and writing, are appropriated by repetition over time. Bodies are shaped, "memory" incorporated, by familiarization through time with movements in space, of eyes or hand, lip or limb; in time and over time, instruction, explanation, commentary become unnecessary. With the habitual skill are incorporated human values and dispositions which, in time and over time, come to be "natural."[10]

These observations apply both to the unspoken rubrics of everyday living and the ceremonial actions of worship. I think of wide-eyed children watching and imitating what they see adults doing in church, sometimes mimicking the preacher's voice or serving their dolls communion. The children's behavior gives witness to some of the more ancient meanings of the word *culture* in the English language: "worship; reverential homage...[and] the training of the human body."[11]

The Necessity of Ritualization

The process of learning these actions is "ritualization," and although we sometimes make disparaging remarks about "empty ritual," ritualization is an inescapable and necessary component of all societies.

> Ritualization is crucial for transmitting agreed-upon rules of conduct; for establishing boundaries between the "good" (the socially sanctioned) and the "bad" (the socially unacceptable); for developing successful social institutions...; and for providing youngsters with adaptive mechanisms that help them enter into the complex symbolic world of adulthood. We become human, Erikson suggested, by learning the ritual repertoire of the human community. Thus, a decay or perversion of effective rituals creates a public and private void– a crisis of meaning and value–that may lead to violence or rage. When a culture loses "the gift of imparting values by meaningful ritualization," Erikson warned, the result is neurosis, social disorder, chaos and conflict.[12]

Churches are under stress because they are nowadays called to minister in a society of multiple cultures and hence multiple ritual traditions. The process of ritualization has become less clear and cohesive, and church leaders feel the resulting "neurosis, social disorder, chaos and conflict."

Consider the "sacrament" or "ordinance" or "memorial" of "the Lord's supper" or "communion" or "eucharist." The variety of names alone suggests something of the multiple cultures that have accumulated around this ritual meal. I have had scores of ministers tell me that with the decline in denominational loyalties, they often have in the same congregation

- some members who have been taught to walk forward to an altar, kneel, make the sign of the cross and hold up their hands to receive the host and the chalice from the celebrant
- some members who have always sat in a pew and taken bread and grape juice from a tray passed to them by ushers
- some members who have always stood in a circle passing bread and wine to one another.

These varied traditions can exercise as profound a grip on people's hearts and minds as my parents' teaching about how to eat noodles. I recall a man who grew up serving as an altar boy in the Roman Catholic Church. After marriage he began to attend church with his wife in the Protestant tradition of which she was a member. Following the communion service one Sunday, the man was enraged to find the deacons emptying the small glasses of unused grape juice down the sink drain and throwing out the leftover cubes of bread that had turned stale. There was no Protestant explanation in the world that could calm his fury. Even though he had long since left the Roman Catholic Church, he still carried in his heart what the priests had taught him as an altar boy: He was to honor the consecrated host and wine as the very body and blood of Christ. Rational theological argument could not displace the man's earlier ritualization.

A range of sacramental practice is just one example of the stress common to today's pluralistic congregations. Sustaining a coherent, meaningful life of worship in a congregation becomes even more complex as we deal with the different musical cultures that people bring with them to worship, both historic traditions of hymnody and more recent popular song, and the different communication styles that now exist in a wired world.

Ritual Pluralism as a Historic Reality in the Church

How can ministers negotiate the pluralism of cultures represented in the larger society and now flooding into the church? This is a question that absorbs the energy of a growing number of pastors. "Numerous Euro-American pastors serve multicultural congregations, and many clergy of various ethnicities occupy cross-cultural pastoral positions. Issues...often arise when the assumed worship practices of the pastor are those of a different cultural orientation than those of the congregation. In such situations, ministry is hindered."[13]

Our era is not the first time in history in which the question of how to minister with and to pluralistic congregations has arisen. During the patristic age, Christians often responded by claiming that their worship represented the universal practices of the church. But in truth they wrote out of the limitations of their own experience and culture.

Authoritative-sounding statements therefore need to be taken with a pinch of salt. When some early Christian author proudly proclaims, for example, that a certain psalm or canticle is sung "throughout the world," it probably means at the most that he knows it to be used in the particular regions he has visited or heard about: it remains an open question whether a similar usage obtained in other parts of the world. Similarly, when some ancient bishop solemnly affirms that a certain liturgical custom is "unheard of" in any church, he is almost certainly excluding from his definition of "church" those groups of Christians whom he judges to be heretical and among whom the practice might well still be flourishing as it once had done in many other places in earlier times, in spite of our bishop's confident (though ignorant) assertion to the contrary.[14]

Another common strategy for stemming the tide of multicultural influences is to appeal to the Bible as if it were insulated from the impact of such forces. But this strategy fails because of the pluralism that the Bible embodies. While giving special attention to the Old Testament and the ancient Near East, Othmar Keel states what is true of the entire biblical canon:

> We now see the Bible imbedded in a broad stream of traditions of the most diverse kind and provenance. Only when this rich environment has been systematically included in the study of the OT do OT conventionalities and originalities clearly emerge. It then becomes evident where the biblical texts are carried by the powerful current of traditions in force for centuries, and where they give an intimation of a new energy inherently their own.[15]

We encounter similar complexities if we attempt to make the New Testament church our model for what worship ought to be in every time and place. "In a sense, it is misleading to speak of the New Testament church; rather, it is more accurate to speak of the churches of the New Testament. The New Testament reveals not one form of worship but several. Distinctions in worship forms existed among the early Aramaic-speaking community, the Hellenistic Jewish community, the early Gentile community, and the sub-apostolic period."[16] Furthermore, those passages that allude to the worship practices of the early church provide only hints and glimpses, and they tend to raise more questions than they answer.

The apostle Paul had to deal with the clash of cultures, not the least of which being between Jew and Gentile. His congregations were in constant jeopardy of splitting apart over a wide range of questions:

- Should they eat food dedicated to idols?
- Whose gifts were to be most valued?
- Was it necessary for males to be circumcised?

Through two millennia cultural differences have continued to stalk the unity of the church, resulting in fierce conflicts over worship and preaching as believers have offered diametrically opposed answers to questions central to their life together:

- Should the church allow images in its worship space?
- Is music so enticing that it draws the church away from prayer?
- Are ceremonial actions of bowing, making the sign of the cross, kneeling, and liturgical dance contrary to the pure spirit of worship?
- Does the use of extended metaphor make preaching too poetical?
- Does it distort the gospel if the preacher is emotionally unrestrained?
- Can women exercise authority and leadership equal to that of male clergy?
- Does one culture more perfectly represent the religious practices ordained by God than another culture?

This list is only a sampling of major conflicts that have marked the history of the church's worship and preaching.

Paul formulates theological principles for holding together culturally diverse congregations, principles that the church has sometimes ignored and sometimes embodied: "Now there are varieties of gifts, but the same Spirit" (1 Cor. 12:4). "Faith, hope, and love abide, these three; and the greatest of these is love" (1 Cor. 13:13). "There is no longer Jew or Greek, there is no longer slave or free, there is no longer male and female; for all of you are one in Christ Jesus" (Gal. 3:28).

No matter how compelling his theology, Paul still finds it necessary to fuse theological principle with practical, pastoral instruction. Paul begins to shape a new culture, an ecclesial culture that will be hospitable to the diverse groups that constitute his fledgling congregations: "Was anyone at the time of his call already circumcised? Let him not seek to remove the marks of circumcision. Was anyone at the time of his call uncircumcised? Let him not seek circumcision" (1 Cor. 7:18). "If food is a cause of [some church members'] falling, I will never eat meat, so that I may not cause one of them to fall" (1 Cor. 8:13). "Since you are eager for spiritual gifts, strive to excel in them for building up the church" (1 Cor. 14:12). "All things should be done decently and in order" (1 Cor. 14:40).

Like Paul, we need a combination of theological principle, cultural awareness, and pastoral wisdom in order to negotiate the pluralism of cultures represented in the larger society and now flooding into the church. We need an ecclesial culture that is hospitable to diversity without losing the distinctive character of the gospel. *Gospel* here does not mean a particular writing, as in "the gospel of Matthew," but rather, the very heart of the good news, the revelation through Jesus Christ of "God's unconditional love for each and every created entity" and God's "will for justice."[17]

Unlike Paul, we have the advantage of a perspective spanning two thousand years of church history and the contributions of ritual and liturgical studies, homiletics, and the social sciences. These are resources that can help us analyze and make critical judgments about the possibilities and liabilities of the various cultures in which our people live. For as liturgists and preachers, one of our necessary roles is to decide what is and is not appropriate in the preaching of the gospel and the worship of the church.

Health and Pathology in Cultures under Transition

My colleague's observation that "Culture is to human beings as water is to fish" implies that we cannot survive without the ability to distinguish between what is healthy and what is pathological in a culture. As long as water is pure and filled with sufficient oxygen and food, fish thrive. But if the water becomes polluted, if the oxygen level is suppressed by toxins, and if the food supply decreases, the very element that gives them life turns against them. It can make them ill or even kill them.

The same is true of the culture in which we live. None of us can afford to live uncritically in the culture that surrounds us. We need some way of testing its purity and toxicity, some way of making clear judgments about what we are ingesting, some way of achieving a degree of objectivity about things that we otherwise take for granted.

History is marked by major shifts in culture, times when all of a sudden human beings felt like fish out of water because the assumed values and meanings of their lives were radically challenged by new discoveries, new perspectives, new revelations. The grip of culture is so strong that people will often refuse, at least initially, to grant the truth of new knowledge. "No person is emotionally indifferent to his culture. Certain cultural premises may become totally out of accord with a new factual situation. Leaders may recognize this and reject the old ways in theory. Yet their emotional loyalty continues in face of reason because of the intimate conditionings of early childhood."[18]

Sigmund Freud claimed that humanity's sense of self-worth as defined by Western religious culture "has been three times severely wounded by the researches of science: the Copernican revolution, Darwin's theory of evolution, and [Freud's] insight into the shadowed depths of the human psyche."[19] Whether or not we are Freudians and whether or not we appreciate his hubris, Freud's comment suggests that three of the primary functions of a culture are to provide

- a sense of location in the universe
- a sense of what it means to participate in human society
- a sense of who we are as feeling, thinking, bodily persons

Ecclesial culture has long embraced these concerns. Consider, for example, the catechism in the Episcopal *Book of Common Prayer*. It outlines basic tenets of the Christian faith, understandings that are common to nearly every Christian tradition and that most churches reinforce continually through preaching and worship:

- As to our location in the universe: "We are part of God's creation."
- As to our participation in society: God intends for us "to live in harmony with creation and with God."
- As to who we are as feeling, thinking, bodily persons: We are "made in the image of God."

The discoveries of Copernicus, Darwin, and Freud appeared initially to challenge these basic affirmations. It would take generations of theological thinking and religious practice to reformulate ecclesial culture so that it was no longer threatened by these discoveries. But their initial impact was devastating. Finding out that the earth is not the center of the universe called into question the significance of human existence. Learning that we were descended from forms of life that we judged inferior shook humanity's dignity and faith in the hand of a benevolent creator. Confronting the obsessive and neurotic aspects of human personality called into question the holy origins of the human soul.

Preachers have often attacked new discoveries that challenged the culture of the church. It is sobering for thoughtful Christians to examine the history of reactions based on theological fear. We do not in our day want to reject truth simply because it does not conform to the theological culture in which we have been raised. Good and holy things often have flowed from major dislocations in the culture. The Copernican revolution eventually resulted in space exploration and satellites that provide more accurate forecasts so that communities can prepare for destructive storms. Darwin's theory of evolution fed biological research that in turn led to great advances in medicine and the saving of millions of lives. Freud's insights touched off a continuing harvest of psychological understandings that have nurtured many healing therapies, including the art of pastoral care. If the church's resistance to these cultural dislocations had prevailed, it would have blocked the Spirit of God from moving through the insights of some of our greatest thinkers.

On the other hand, not every change in culture is a revelation of truth. Even those shifts in culture that are based on important new data and theories carry with them the potential for distortion and misuse. The same transformations that bring us good and holy gifts often result as well in what is sinful and wrong. Thus, for example, the scientific revolution in which Copernicus participated also objectified creation in ways that have subsequently led to the abuse of nature through overdevelopment and pollution. The Darwinian insights about evolution were transmuted into social theories of the survival of the fittest to justify huge discrepancies between the wealthy and the poor. Freud's contributions to our understanding of the human psyche have sometimes fed a preoccupation with the self and the disavowal of ethical responsibility.

The advent of a wired world, what Neil Postman terms "Technopoly," may now represent another major cultural dislocation.[20] Technopoly for Postman is more than the sum total of our electronic devices and interconnected media. Technopoly is a way of being and doing. Technopoly is a culture that engages our senses and shapes our thinking and self-expression. I think, for example, of my in-laws, who are in their nineties. They have remarked several times to my wife and me how when they have a question about a bill, no longer is there an address of someone to whom they can write a letter. The only option is a phone number (that will be answered by an electronic device) or a Web site. They are baffled and sometimes overwhelmed by this new electronic world. To them it is a foreign culture. However, to the generation raised on PCs and cell phones, it is home territory.

As in the cases of Copernicus, Darwin, and Freud, the transforming impact of technopoly is a mixed blessing. The possibilities for research, learning, communication, creativity, and advances in every field—including the mission and ministry of the church—are immense. But technopoly also brings distortions, losses, and the dangers of self-illusion to the human community, because

> in Technopoly, all experts are invested with the charisma of priestliness. Some of our priest-experts are called psychia-trists, some psychologists, some sociologists, some statisti-cians. The god they serve does not speak of righteousness or goodness or mercy or grace. Their god speaks of efficiency,

precision, objectivity. And that is why such concepts as sin and evil disappear in Technopoly. They come from a moral universe that is irrelevant to the theology of expertise. And so the priests of Technopoly call sin "social deviance," which is a statistical concept, and they call evil "psychopathology," which is a medical concept. Sin and evil disappear because they cannot be measured and objectified, and therefore cannot be dealt with by experts.[21]

Neither Fear nor Acquiescence

How, then, do preachers relate to the emergence of what is new in a culture while maintaining a critical perspective? How do we neither react out of fear nor collapse into faithless acquiescence?

We who preach and lead worship cannot escape these questions. Every time we use a current movie or news item or novel or work of art or popular song in a sermon or service, we are negotiating the complex relationship between our theology and the culture in which our people live. Every time we meet with a worship committee to consider how to vitalize our liturgies, we join the dialogue between the gospel and culture that has persisted throughout the history of the church.

What are the unique resources of homiletics and liturgics that can help us relate faithfully to the culture so that we affirm what is true, good, and beautiful, while we offer a discerning judgment about what is false, wrong, and ugly? Like Paul, we need theological acumen and practical, pastoral wisdom in order to be faithful to the movement of the Spirit in our own time and cultures.

Developing a Grid for Cultural Analysis

Because the range of materials church leaders have to deal with is so diverse and complex, I propose a grid to help us understand the profile of a culture by charting the most characteristic features of its communal rituals. The grid is my attempt to help us visualize a culture's sensorium. It is based on five questions that we have already identified as implicit in the traditions and practices of all cultures.

- How will we use our eyes?
- How will we use our ears?
- How will we use our bodies?
- How will we use language?
- What is the meaning of how we use eyes, ears, bodies, and language?

There are, of course, more than five dimensions to plotting something as complex as a culture! In limiting our discussion to five, we realize that "full or exhaustive knowledge [of a culture] is not easy to come by, and we are a long way from it at present. But to say we are far from knowing all about the sensorium is not to say we know nothing about it."[22] A grid based on these five questions provides a manageable way of gaining the general profile of a culture, a way of charting some of its most salient characteristics.

I have placed the questions of language and meaning last on the grid because preachers and liturgists usually turn to them first. The tendency to begin with a consideration of language and meaning sometimes keeps us from seeing that many of our cultural conflicts are about different ways of being, acting, and sensing. Our difficulties arise from our material differences, not simply from our words. Scholars involved in cultural analysis have themselves been shifting "from what Lawrence Sullivan has called an 'overly literary' approach to religion, to a reorientation toward the material practices and dimensions of religions."[23]

Preachers, whose preeminent concern is language, need a keener awareness of how "our senses are historically and socially organized. Our senses are conditioned and influenced by the period of time in which we live and the cultures of which we are a part. This means that our sight, hearing, smell, touch, and taste are shaped by our lives as social and historical beings."[24]

Furthermore, focusing on words alone ignores how preaching is itself a ritual act that takes place in a ritual context. We end up with verbal reductionism, when in fact the way a congregation responds to a sermon is significantly shaped by the other ritual factors, a phenomenon we will be tracing in later chapters.

Verbal reductionism also distorts our understanding of history and the nonverbal resources that history can provide for understanding our current struggles with the relationship between church and culture. "Non-language users are frequently ignored by historians; they are often considered incapable of providing interesting or usable antecedents for modern subjective consciousness...And yet the lives of non-language users were no less ordered by ideas and images than were those of language users."[25]

"Meaning" is the last category on the grid. Generally speaking, we who are comfortable with language assume that meaning arises from reflective thought. In fact, however, the physical and mental are not nearly so isolated from each other as our reason often tricks us into believing. "It is not so easy to draw a clear line between impulses whose motivation comes from the body and the more abstract directives that arise from the mind and brain. As in the human person, there is a constant interplay between the physical and cognitive, or reflective dimension of consciousness. This interaction between conscious and impulsive processes of thought can be observed in culture as a whole."[26]

When we neglect the interplay of the physical and the mental, we distort our understanding of where and why certain worship practices have arisen. I recall, for example, a seminary student serving a church whose liturgy opened with a procession down the middle aisle of the nave led by someone bearing a cross atop a high pole. When the crucifer was about three quarters down the aisle, he would bend his knees, almost squatting as he walked the last few steps to the chancel. Then he would resume an upright posture to position the cross in a stand next to the altar. The seminary student, intrigued by this strange action, asked around in the congregation about its meaning and always received the same answer: "It is our way of showing honor to Christ as represented by the altar."

Several months later an old man visited the service and broke into laughter upon seeing the crucifer squat and walk. After the service, the visitor explained that as a little boy he had attended this church, and at that time there was a low gothic arch in front of the altar. The crucifer had taken to the squatting position in order not to bang the arch with the cross. In the years since the old man had left the congregation, the nave had been remodeled, taking out the gothic arch. But the ritual had continued! The theology was secondary to the action. The church had developed its own rationale, its own meaning, to support an inherited gesture.

Here are a few of the major functions and meanings commonly ascribed to rituals that arise from the unceasing interplay between body and mind, physical space and reflection, materiality and consciousness:

> to bring the uncontrollable, such as rainfall, into relation with the controlled, such as ploughing and sowing,...[to carry on] the transmission of culturally vital information,...[to provide] a means of expressing the collective consciousness of a group through the enacted reinforcement of social structure,...[to] remove anxiety and resentment through catharsis,...to contradict the world as lived by immersing the body in a larger process of Becoming,...to mediate beneath the level of surface meaning.[27]

The same ritual, depending on culture, may function in different ways and carry multiple meanings. Think, for example, of the varied interpretations and functions that Christians have historically ascribed to baptism and eucharist, a pluralism of understandings that is heightened by the current nature of people's wandering church allegiances: "With the erosion of denominational and other affiliative ties, mainline American Christians increasingly seek a congregation where they are 'at home' or feel that they 'belong.' Consequently, it is not at all uncommon for a person to belong to a Methodist congregation in one community, to join a Presbyterian church in another, and to worship with the Baptists in a third."[28]

Here now is the grid that helps us plot how sensoria differ from culture to culture. I use my experience in the Japanese noodle shop

JAPANESE				
eye	**ear**	**body**	**language**	**meaning**
Direct eye contact is rare during conversation	Ear detects sound of eating noodles	Bowing to greet me, often bowing during conversation Body bent toward table More rapid use of arm and hand movements while eating Audibly sucking noodles Nodding of head affirmatively during conversation	More indirection in expressing contrary views Lower dynamic level with less dramatic tonal changes	Provide nourishment to the body Enjoy food through both taste and sound of ingesting it Provide and accept hospitality with expressed gratitude Maintain contact during conversation even when disagreeing

AMERICAN				
eye	**ear**	**body**	**language**	**meaning**
Much more direct eye contact during conversation	Ear cannot detect sound of eating	Offering right hand in greeting Not bowing during conversation Discreet twirling of noodles with slower motion of arm and hand Nearly silent consumption of noodles Head mostly held still Sit straight, no elbows on table	More direct statement of one's position Greater shifts in dynamic level and pitch (This may only seem to be the case because of how my ears are trained)	Provide nourishment to the body Enjoy food by taste but not sound Provide and accept hospitality with expressed gratitude Convince others of the truth of one's position when it differs from theirs

to illustrate how persons of different cultures use their eyes, ears, bodies, and language to create meaning. The goal is not to judge one culture as better than the other, but to chart their characteristic ways of acting and being.

I have applied the grid to the relatively neutral case of different eating rituals to clarify my principles for analyzing the interrelationship of worship, preaching, and culture. Without such clarity it is easy to jump to premature judgments about a particular practice, denying the theological validity and spiritual insight of a custom when in truth what it represents is simply a difference in culture.

In the case of the noodle shop experience the need for nourishment and the mutual desire to provide and receive hospitality were the dominant shared functions and meanings of our time together. They were so important to everyone that it was easy to accept the different table rituals and even to laugh about them with one another.

But imagine for a moment that my Japanese friends and I begin meeting every Sunday, and we consider our noodle eating to be a sacrament instituted by God. All of a sudden the stakes are much higher. The meal is no longer a single occasion. It has become a ritual, a repeated action. We need to figure out how we will handle our differences. At least four possible solutions come immediately to mind:

Solution Number One. We decide to let the sound-making noodle eaters and the silent noodle eaters continue according to their own custom. The advantage is that we honor one another's culture. The disadvantage is that we lose the sense of group cohesiveness that a single ritual practice provides, and we have difficulty ritualizing our children and other newcomers who are confused by the diversity of our practice.

Solution Number Two. We decide that we will all make sounds with our noodles *or* that we will all eat our noodles silently. The advantage is that we gain a single ritual practice that helps us to act as one group, and it is easier to ritualize our children and newcomers. The disadvantage is that we have privileged one culture over the other, and the side whose practice has been dropped feels marginalized.

Solution Number Three. We decide to have two different gatherings, one for the sound-making noodle eaters and one for the silent noodle eaters. The advantage is that people now feel at home in the ritual they attend, and their resistance to practices different from their own no longer lessens the effectiveness of the ritual. The disadvantage is that we have now created two separate communities, and we lose the richness, of intercultural exchange and the way that exchange broadens our understanding of the world.

Solution Number Four. We start serving popcorn instead of noodles so that all the participants eat with their hands, using neither chopsticks nor utensils. The advantage is that we are no longer divided into sound-making noodle eaters and silent noodle eaters. The disadvantage is that we feel cut off from our historic roots, the symbolic richness, and the divine mandate that made our ceremonial eating together a sacrament.

The different ways the two cultures employ language further complicate the negotiations for an acceptable solution. The sound-making noodle eaters use forms of indirect communication offered in well-modulated tones, while the silent noodle eaters argue directly for what they want in inflections that dramatize the force of their convictions.

The tension becomes so great that various noodle eaters give up the ritual all together, while others split off to form their own groups, each claiming to represent the one, true, and holy way of eating noodles.

Because the example of noodle eating is distant from our pressing concerns, it affords us a measure of objectivity and humor. These are the very qualities that we need in our churches but that are most often lacking when we encounter questions that arise from culturally fed disagreements about worship and preaching.

The grid is an instrument to help us trace the deep cultural roots of much that we hold dear. This is the first step in beginning to understand the interrelationship of culture, preaching, and worship. If we skip this critical first step and proceed immediately to theological judgment, we run the risk of absolutizing, in the name of God, that which our culture has created.

All of Us for All of God

The initial step of cultural analysis, though essential, is not by itself adequate for the leadership of a church's worship and preaching. There remains the more complex task of formulating theological judgments. No culture is perfect, and all cultures embody practices that are evil and oppressive as well as good and life-enhancing. Cultures can exist for centuries based on religiously sanctioned prejudices and brutal hierarchies of privilege and power. Because as Christians we believe that the reign of God is breaking in on human affairs, we are obligated to ask critical questions about the culture that surrounds the church as well as the culture that prevails within the church. Just because something is popular or accepted as "standard practice" does not mean it is appropriate to the church's worship and preaching. Every generation of faith and every expansion of the church into new regions is drawn into struggling with these questions:

- What does a culture offer that the church can adapt and use?
- What does a culture offer that the church needs to reject or transform?
- What does a culture offer that corrects the distorted practices and values of the church?

Before we leap to answer these questions for our own time and place in history, it will serve us well to examine how for good—and for ill—the church has made these cultural/theological judgments in the past. To decide what we will embody in the church's worship and preaching only on the basis of our generation's taste and experience is narcissism of the worst sort, dangerous to our health and the health of our children. It brings to mind an imperfectly remembered inscription above a university library: "The generation that knows only itself will remain a child forever." Whatever the culture of our churches, our faith invites us to aspire not to perpetual childhood but to come "to maturity, to the measure of the full stature of Christ" (Eph. 4:13). Our maturity as a church depends on our learning from the last two thousand years of Christian experience, not just the last twenty or forty or eighty.

One way to chart the maturity and immaturity of the church through history is to hold its practices up to the two greatest commandments: love of God and love of neighbor. It is significant that when Jesus is asked to identify "'Which commandment is the first of all?'" (Mk. 12:28), he chooses one from the worship practices of his community. His answer reveals an ability to make cultural judgments, to look at an elaborate network of ritual behaviors and to decide what takes precedence above all the others.

Jesus names as the first and greatest commandment the *Shema* (meaning "hear," in Hebrew). "'Hear, O Israel: the Lord our God, the Lord is one; you shall love the Lord your God with all your heart, and with all your soul, and with all your mind, and with all your strength'" (Mk. 12:29b–30).

The *Shema* is addressed to the corporate body, "Israel." The community is called to bring its entire being into the act of worship. The "heart and mind" connote the joining of will and intellect, while "soul" describes "the vitality of selfhood."[29] The final word, "strength," *ischus* in Greek, includes "strength of body"[30] as well as strength of spirit. Hebrew worship made this last part of the commandment more than a figure of speech. It took strength to play instruments, sing, process, dance, bow, and raise their hands in prayer. As a former colleague of mine used to paraphrase this commandment: "All of us for all of God."[31]

"All of us" includes all that we are as a community and all that each of us is as an individual self. Sometimes we have too constricted an understanding of the self, thinking it is nothing more than our consciousness as a subjective being, but in fact "self" is a much more complex construction. We are shaped not only by our individual, psychological predilections but also by the natural and cultural forces that surround us. "The self includes the body, mind, and spirit; abilities and limitations; and repressed and remembered experiences both positive and negative: bodily experience, relational experience, cultural experience, religious experience."[32]

When we use less than "all of us for all of God," we stand in danger of a distorted spirituality.

> One might suggest that it is where the body and the mind interact that culture becomes most creative and vital. Where spirituality, or religious expression, becomes totally a matter of physical sensations and uncontrolled emotions, we become the prey of irrational forces such as those to be found in fundamentalism. But on the other hand, where faith becomes just a matter of intellectual ideas and abstract formulations, spirituality also degenerates into dogmatism, arid rationalism or individual opinions on this or that issue.[33]

In the gospel of Matthew, Jesus connects the second commandment to the first by using the adjective *homoios,* whose first meaning in Greek is "of the same nature" (Mt. 22:39).[34] Love of God and love of neighbor are "of the same nature." Worship and ethics are interfused. When we give all of us to all of God, our worship and preaching flow into the world as love for our neighbor. Then we embody "the measure of the full stature of Christ." Then the culture of the church becomes a vessel of the living Spirit of God.

Cultural Analysis as a Tool for Understanding Worship and Preaching

Throughout this book I will be drawing on a broad body of literature representing many different disciplines and fields of inquiry. Yet they share in common an attentiveness to cultural analysis. Whether looking at Christian art or the worship practices of the church or the interpretation of scripture, the authors manifest an acute interest in understanding the dialectical relationship between their field of interest and culture. They often employ tools of observation and description that have been developed by the social sciences. Their work is typical of the current "widespread move to cultural and social theory on the part of religious studies scholars…and to the increasing interpretation in the United States of theology as a form of cultural analysis and criticism."[35]

Leonora Tubbs Tisdale has been a leader in demonstrating how pastors can "become amateur cultural anthropologists, studying and interpreting the symbols of congregational life in order to gain greater understanding of congregational subcultural identity."[36] Like myself, Tisdale acknowledges her debt to Robert J. Schreiter, who gives us a theological rationale for the use of cultural analysis. "The development of local theologies depends as much on finding Christ already active in the culture as it does on bringing Christ to the culture. The great respect for culture has a christological basis. It grows out of a belief that the risen Christ's salvific activity in bringing about the kingdom of God is already going on before our arrival."[37]

We undertake this cultural analysis not as objective, value-free observers, but as church leaders with a commitment to the gospel, with a conviction that Christ is risen and living, that Christ is to be found in, among, and through the practices of different cultures, sometimes sustaining them, sometimes calling us to transform them.

The tools of cultural analysis help us understand how the gospel becomes incarnate in a particular culture. Without such awareness, we may rush to judgment against practices that are different from our own without taking time to consider how they may be yet another way of God's presence being manifest in the world.

The Total Human Consciousness of the Divine

Our goal is to understand more of the fullness of God's revelation and being. As William James once put the matter: "Is the existence of so many religious types and sects and creeds regrettable? To these questions I answer 'no' emphatically...If an Emerson were forced to be a Wesley, or a Moody forced to be a Whitman, the total human consciousness of the divine would suffer."[38] Our hope is to expand "the total human consciousness of the divine" in order to lessen the possibility for religious oppression and to expand the realization of religion's healthiest dynamics: reconciliation, doing justice, showing compassion, remaining alive to the new motions of God's living Spirit.

Here is a copy of the blank grid to aid in the work of cultural analysis. I suggest readers make several photocopies, which they can use to analyze their services and sermons, and to contrast them with the practices of others *or* with goals they have for the transformation of their ritual practices.

We employ this grid mindful of people with disabilities that make it impossible for them to use their bodies or senses or speech according to the norms of their culture. Church and society often treat them as less than fully human because they do not function within the prevailing sensorium. Our sermons and our institutions frequently foster injustice by viewing "persons with disabilities as objects to be dealt with, rather than as subjects that have something to contribute."[39] We do not wish to perpetuate the wrong. We hope cultural analysis will help church leaders identify how worship and preaching unwittingly reinforce biases that are antithetical to the gospel. Our

eye	ear	body	language	meaning

analyses will lead us to ask, How do we need to expand the church's culture to include those left out by our prevailing sensorium?

We can also deepen our cultural analysis by considering different periods in the development of the church. Seeing the wisdom and the wrong of the past alerts us to the wisdom and wrong of the present. We look backward to look forward: We draw from history the critical consciousness that empowers us to bring all of us to all of God and to love our neighbors as ourselves.

Understanding the interrelationship of culture, preaching, and worship is, then, more than an intriguing intellectual quest, though it is certainly that. It is a way of our more faithfully following Christ, a way of drawing the church toward a fuller realization of the two greatest commandments, a way of knowing more fully "the depth of the riches and wisdom and knowledge of God" (Rom. 11:33) as they are manifested through a world of vast cultural diversity.

2

EYE

When I was a boy growing up in church, one of the most frequently sung hymns was "Open my eyes, that I may see/Glimpses of truth Thou hast for me."[1] But in practice the Presbyterian, Methodist, and Baptist congregations in which I sang these words were never very hospitable to the use of the eyes in worship. Sometimes there were stained-glass windows, but with the exception of the Good Shepherd or an empty cross, most of them featured geometric shapes bordered by a margin of fleur-de-lis or other heraldic symbol. There were, with a few exceptions, none of the elaborate dramatic scenes from the Bible or the lives of the saints that fill Roman Catholic and Episcopal churches.

The preachers mirrored the austerity of the windows. They either wore a black suit and white shirt with dark tie or a black preacher's gown. Now and then they had a stole draped over their shoulders, but the color was usually a weak lime green, and it was embossed not with a dove or a flame or even a cross but with the Roman letters IHS. The brightest colors I remember from my childhood churches were the flowers, a little taste of Isaiah's promise that the desert will blossom.

Because it was the church culture in which I grew up, I assumed as a child that it was what church always had been and forever would be. Yet whenever I visited the Roman Catholic church with my friend or went to play flute in the Episcopal church, I was aware I had stepped into another world. I intuited as a child what I would later understand as an adult: "Our senses are conditioned and influenced by the period of time in which we live and the cultures of which we are a part. This means that our sight, hearing, smell, touch, and taste are shaped by our lives as social and historical beings."[2] But this is knowledge I would not gain until much later in life. As a child, I was an uncritical inheritor of traditions that arose from John Calvin (1509–1564) and his followers. For Calvin,

> it was simply unthinkable that pictures could have cluttered up [the] pristine spiritual commonwealth [of the apostolic and patristic periods]. And so he concluded there had been none, no pictures in Christian churches before Chalcedon (451 C.E.). Primitive Christianity had been an aniconic form of religiosity…This sixteenth-century view of the early church is quintessentially a product of the Calvinist branch of the Reformation. And it has exercised a profound influence on all later historical reconstructions of the early Christian attitudes toward art, not least in our own century.[3]

The Roots of Protestant Iconoclasm

The iconoclasm of Calvin and his followers was not necessarily an opposition to visual images in themselves. They rejected such images because they were associated with liturgical practices that their new theologies condemned. To accept visual images was to open the door to what the Calvinists considered unbiblical and therefore corrupt practices. They particularly abhorred the spectacle of dramatized liturgies that characterized some late medieval services. The dramatic actions were

> intended to make the liturgy's meaning plain to lay people. For example, on Ascension Thursday the ascent of Christ into heaven was dramatized by drawing up through a hole in the church roof a figure of Christ, and afterwards a rag doll coated with pitch was tossed down through the hole to represent the defeat of the Devil. Similarly on Whitsun, a dove was lowered from the roof to symbolize the descent of the Holy Spirit. Crucifixes featured prominently in the liturgy, as well as the *Olberg,* strictly speaking a representation of Christ's passion in the garden of Gethsemane, often formed from statuary and set up outdoors in the churchyard. To this

was sometimes added a Holy Sepulchre, used in the Easter liturgy, and a Calvary scene...

Attacks on the images of the *Olberg* occurred fairly frequently, and we could see them as attacks on the liturgy with which it was associated. In the same way, attacks on the crucifix were also attacks on the doctrine of the real presence of Christ in the Eucharist. The crucifix was closely associated with this doctrine because of the way it was used in the liturgy in the place of the consecrated host.[4]

The Protestant iconoclasts were responding to practices that their Roman Catholic opponents also sought to correct. Both parties recognized "an imbalance between engagement of the visual sense and of the auditory sense of the worshipper" so that people were "not expected or trained to use ears and discursive intellect, but only eyes and emotion in worship."[5]

The failure to engage the ear while overemphasizing the eye left the late medieval church with a lopsided piety. Tragically, the different parties who perceived the distortion were not able to achieve a common understanding of how to correct what they knew was wrong. Each developed an ecclesial culture with a different prevailing sensorium, and they became violently hostile to one another. The ensuing religious wars are a reminder that the collision of cultures can release violent forces, even when those cultures share the name of Christ.

There were also political, economic, and nationalistic factors that fed those horrific wars, but we must never underrate the significance of their conflicts over worship. The way people enact their religious understandings through worship has the potential to feed hatred as well as love, and we need to make sure the whole church remembers this when we begin to struggle with the issues of contemporary worship.

Images on the Page Versus Images in Church

Although distressed at the liturgical associations of many late medieval images, the reformers realized the usefulness of images in planting faith in people's hearts.

Luther believed as much as pre-Reformation teachers that images were valuable means of instruction. As he put it in 1522: "children and simple folk...are more easily moved by pictures and images to recall divine history than through

mere words or doctrines." Thus he favored the use of illustrated Bibles and Catechisms, and other illustrated religious
books: only that the pictures should be consistent with right
evangelical belief and the Word of God.[6]

There is, however, a significant difference between a picture in a
book and an image such as a statue or stained-glass window that
commands the attention of an entire worshiping assembly. The book
changes the way the image functions: It now becomes something
viewed by the isolated individual. The shift of the eye from the
surrounding environment of the worship space to the page brings an
enormous cultural transformation. Protestants become "people of the
book." Looking at a book is different from looking at an image that
fills public space. The eyes and generally the shoulders move
downward so that the individual becomes more encapsulated, thus
losing the sense of community that results from looking up and out
with other worshipers at the same image. The change in visual focus
changes the use of the body, and the new use of the body changes the
nature of the community and its culture.

Calvinistic reformers did not abandon the eye altogether. That
would have required worshiping with blinders on! Instead, they
reduced the amount of visual stimulation. Anyone who has ever
worshiped in a New England meeting house will remember the clear
glass windows, the white walls, the minimal use of symbols: usually a
high pulpit, a baptismal font, a table, and possibly a simple empty
cross. The effect of light and simplicity in a well-proportioned room
can itself be a stunning visual experience, and it can powerfully
symbolize the light and clarity of God and God's Word. It is a way of
employing the eye, but it is very different from late medieval visual
culture.

I recall being in a plain church in a museum that featured an
early American village. There was a curator who explained the history
of the church. When he finished, a person who identified himself as
Roman Catholic asked, "But what did they do with their eyes?" Several
Protestants, accustomed to a plain worship space, responded: "What
do you mean, 'What did they do with their eyes?'" Different ecclesial
cultures had taught them different ways of seeing in worship.

Nowadays the growing use of PowerPoint and video images in
the "contemporary worship" of many Protestant churches may be a
form of returning to late medieval visual culture. One way to
understand the phenomenon is to see it as an attempt to rebalance
the lopsided piety of Protestant worship that resulted when the ear

displaced the eye, when hearing and reading ascended to the dominant position that public images had once commanded.

The Oscillating Sensorium of the Church

The Protestant movements transformed the sensorium of the church. Champions of the new culture arose to vaunt its superior values. For example, the Christian humanist scholar Erasmus (probably 1469–1536) writes in *The Manual of the Christian Knight*:

> You honour the image of the bodily countenance of Christ formed in stone or wood or else portrayed with colours. With much greater reverence is to be honoured the image of his mind, which by workmanship of the Holy Ghost is figured and expressed in the Gospels.[7]

The reformations of the sixteenth century were not the first Christian movements that held images suspect. The use of the eye in worship is marked by a history of oscillation as Christians sometimes favored, sometimes outlawed the use of images. Long before the reformations of the 1500s, the church periodically attempted to suppress or control the use of images in worship.

> In 691, for example, the well-known canon 82 of the Council in Trullo forbade the representation of Christ as a lamb or otherwise in symbolic form; he was to be depicted only in human form, so that "we may recall to memory his conversation in the flesh, his passion and salutary death and his redemption which was wrought for the whole world."[8]

There was by no means unanimous agreement about this edict. It was, instead, part of a strenuous debate between those who favored and those who opposed the use of images.

> In Byzantium, both the pro- and anti-image factions culled their quotations from the same patristic sources, and both did so with equal disregard for the original literary and historical contexts that defined their materials. Both arranged their excerpted materials polemically, and for both the goal was the same, namely to prove that the authoritative testimony of a given excerpt represented the true line of Christian tradition, both in thought and in practice.[9]

And sometimes we think that wars over worship are a phenomenon unique to our generation!

Issues surrounding the appropriate use of the eye in the life of faith emerge again and again in the church's history. The visual media may shift, but the debate keeps erupting. Thus, for example, the advent and rapid spread of movies occasioned immense struggles over the appropriateness of using this medium to communicate the gospel. There was in Great Britain during the 1920s and 1930s opposition to

> the representation of sacred persons on film. It might have been thought that Christ would have been permitted more easily than God, as he had been so frequently depicted by painters...By 1939 the question of sacred portrayals on stage and screen was still a difficult matter which would be subject to further consideration and controversy.[10]

Just as the church of ancient Byzantium was divided over images, so too the church in Great Britain. While some believers resisted, others championed the new visual medium of the cinema as an opportunity, even a mandate, for presenting the gospel in fresh ways. "The Revd Albert Peel, later a chairman of the Congregational Union, wrote in 1936 that the Church should devote all her resources to the production and distribution of good films: 'the Church will be failing her Lord if she fails to baptize this magnificent instrument into the service of His kingdom.'"[11]

The Bible Used to Support and Attack Images

Whether we are dealing with the ancient church or the modern era, the community of faith goes back and forth between affirming and denying the place of visual images in the life of faith. The oscillation arises in large part from the Bible's ambivalence about images. We are commanded not to make images of God, yet scripture presents us with a plethora of imaginative visions of the deity, describes the temple as a richly decorated interior space (1 Kings 6:14–37), and names Christ to be "the image of the invisible God" (Col. 1:15).

Opponents and proponents of the use of images can each find passages to support their positions. An appeal to the Bible has never conclusively settled the matter. But that has not kept people from trying!

Minucius Felix (second or third century C.E.) writes a defense of Christianity in the form of a conversation between two fictional characters: Ocatavius, who is Christian, and Caecilius, who is pagan. Among the things that Octavius explains is why Christians do not need "material props to support worship, including one of the central cult objects within traditional Greek religion, namely the sacred image.

The interior disposition of the worshiper is all that counts. God lives in the mind and heart of the individual and what matters to God is an honest heart *(bonus animus)*, a pure mind *(pura mens)*, and a clear conscience *(sincera sententia)*."[12]

Drawing on the thought of Plato, Clement of Alexandria concluded that images belong to the lower world of material existence, characterized by shadow and illusion. Clement believed that any representation of the invisible God was a lie. He classified the making of such objects "as a form of thievery, because the sculptor and the painter steal the truth *(aletheia)* from God. Using their mimetic skills, they pretend to make animals and plants, but this false and deceptive appropriation is nothing more than Robbery...Truth, by contrast, belongs to the upper world, the noetic realm, which Middle Platonists denominated under *logos epistemikos,* pure or true knowledge."[13]

Clement and Minucius Felix, through his fictional character Octavius, sensed what a later art historian identifies as the danger of images, a danger that appears especially threatening to those whose primary means of expression is written language. "The translation of the Gospels from Greek into Latin altered their content only very marginally; the translation of the Gospels from literature into visual images profoundly affected their content...Images are dangerous. Images, no matter how discreetly chosen, come freighted with conscious or subliminal memories; no matter how limited their projected use, they burn indelible outlines into the mind."[14]

Images as Access to the Divine

Visual images can be dangerous: To put matters this strongly is to enter more deeply into the nature of the culture wars that are always raging in church and society. When people sense danger, they do not respond with detachment or with careful analysis. They respond with a creature's instincts for survival. All of a sudden we find ourselves fighting to protect our territory because we feel that if we lose it, we ourselves will be lost. Historical cultural analysis can help us make sounder decisions about worship and preaching in our own day. We can learn from our ancestors in the faith, observing when they responded in panic and when they responded faithfully and creatively to new developments. Their stories remind us not to make premature judgments against expressions of the gospel whose means of communication are foreign to us.

The ancient debates about images reveal that no amount of theological opposition, ecclesial authority, and biblical citation is sufficient to suppress the need of the human heart for visualizing the holy. The power that makes images dangerous also makes them popular. While theologians debated the pros and cons of an iconic Christianity, the appeal among believers of images expressing the gospel "was universal: a good deal of contemporary anecdotal evidence suggests that they were seen by high and low alike as offering the power of emotional solace and access to the divine."[15]

The phrases "emotional solace" and "access to the divine" give us yet another key to understanding the depth and the passion we feel for any particular cultural practice that we consider to be holy. Surely one of the greatest attractions of the gospel is the "emotional solace" that it brings to our fractured and frequently tragic lives. If a particular hymn or prayer or ritual action or image or altar or statue has been a source of "emotional solace" to us throughout our lives, we will feel threatened if it is removed or altered. It may seem as though the nervous system has been ripped out of our soul. We do not care how many explanations we hear for why our favorite hymn is not in the new book or why the altar is being replaced or why the stained-glass window is removed to make room for the door required by fire inspectors.

The familiarity of the symbol may increase its power. It can give us "access to the divine" because it does not require elaborate cognitive processing. There it is, week after week; year after year; through baptisms, weddings, and funerals; through the seasons of penance and the joy of Christmas, Eastertide, and Pentecost. The associations with the holy are so deep and reliable that the beloved sacred image draws us immediately into relationship with God, Christ, Spirit.

There is, for example, in the church of which I am a member, a deep blue stained-glass window featuring an image of the crucified and resurrected Christ in a contrasting robe of the richest imaginable red, his wounded hands crossed in a gesture of prayer. The window fills the upper chancel above the altar. Visitors to the church often remark that this image and the surrounding windows are among the most beautiful they have ever seen.

I find that every time I enter the church before worship, I kneel and pray with my eyes fixed on the risen Christ with the wounded hands. Prayer flows with an intensity and focus that prepares me as nothing else for the corporate worship that is about to begin. The windows are not God, but they provide "access to the divine."

Over the years, I have discovered in conversation with other members of the congregation that mine is not an isolated response. There are many worshipers for whom the image of the risen Christ functions in the same way. What I have learned from this is that the culture of our particular congregation is shaped, informed, and even defined to a significant degree by the impact of the deep blue window with the image of Christ. Since all symbols are polyvalent, the image undoubtedly functions in different ways for different viewers, but the most common theme I pick up from people is how the window gives them a sense of the risen, living Christ. The window does not argue us into belief. Instead, it invites us into prayer, so that we find ourselves in the presence of Christ. The doctrine of the resurrection becomes less a teaching of the church and more a reality that we encounter here and now. We experience what many Christians of late antiquity began to realize, when

> religious images began to be seen as a means of demonstrating doctrine even more exactly than could be done in words; their potential in this regard is explicitly defended in the powerful argument put by Anastasius of Sinai [600s C.E.]… according to which pictures are a more effective way of convincing people of true doctrine than quotations from the Scripture and the Fathers.[16]

The Image Mightier than the Sword

Sometimes it has been not the pen nor the word but the image that is mightier than the sword. This is true not just for the ancients but for many Christians raised in our own era. In a fascinating reflection on her Roman Catholic upbringing, the contemporary writer and novelist Mary Gordon explains that the Bible

> was not something you wrote about, or even anything you read: it was what you heard…it was a story that had nothing to do with history or print. We did not read the Bible; we were Catholics…Inevitable, like the seasons, were certain narrative events. The Passion, of course, and Christmas, the Ascension, Pentecost; but the stories took on the flavor of certain weathers…The Gospels appeared to me as scenes.[17]

The Roman Catholic culture of her childhood that Gordon describes has changed significantly since Vatican II and Pope John XXIII. The Roman lectionary and its offspring, the common lectionary (the cooperative work of Roman Catholic and Protestant scholars), increased attention to homiletics—all this resulted in lessening the difference between the biblical culture of Protestant worship and the visual, sensual culture that Gordon vividly recalls.

Many Protestant denominations whose histories have been primarily text-oriented and often aniconic find themselves struggling with how to visualize their worship. It may be that the "imbalance between engagement of the visual sense and of the auditory sense of the worshipper"[18] that haunted the late medieval church is now–five centuries later!–finally beginning to be righted. What was impossible for either Protestants or Roman Catholics to do under the stress of the political, social, and cultural pressures of the 1500s may in our age have a greater chance of realization. If, however, the supervisualized world of the electronic media comes to dominate our liturgies, then our worship may once again lack the balance that results when text and speech complement image and dramatic action.

Tex Sample demonstrates the power of electronic images through a conversation with his fourteen-year-old granddaughter about a rock video of a particular song. Sample asks what the group is singing about, and the granddaughter responds: "'I don't know, Grandpa, I never listen to the words…I hear them, but I just don't pay attention to them.'"[19] If this happens in worship, we might end up repeating the distortions of the late medieval church, when people listened to Latin, a language they did not speak or read. Knowing the language was not necessary, because they were "not expected or trained to use ears and discursive intellect, but only eyes and emotion in worship."[20] If we take that route in our own age, worship will not engage all of us for all of God, but only part of us for part of God.

The Irrepressible Hunger for Images

There appears to be an irrepressible need in the hearts of most believers for visualization of the holy to provide "emotional solace and access to the divine." Even people who dismiss visual images as idols often turn to language that is highly imagistic. Consider, for example, the Puritan minister Edward Taylor, a man keenly aware and committed in principle to the Calvinistic stricture against all forms of idolatry. Despite those convictions, "The erotic, anthropomorphic nature of the images [in Taylor's poetry] suggests a strong personal need to visualize God in corporeal form."[21] Straining to repress the graphic representation of God, the need for images erupts into language. Taylor rhapsodizes about a maternal Christ who offers solace to the soul, saying,

> Peace, Peace, my Hony, do not Cry,
> My Little Darling, wipe thine eyes,
> Oh Cheer, Cheer up, come see.

Is anything too deare, my Dove,
Is anything too good, my Love
To get or give for thee?[22]

The Puritans, whose official theological position was stringently anti-iconic, in fact used images not just in their language but in their material art as well, particularly in their graveyards. "Puritan tombstones offer the most explicit evidence of American Puritans' need to create graven images. Only forty years after they arrived on this side of the Atlantic, Puritans began to carve onto their gravestones the images of 'things in heaven above' that were forbidden in their churches–angels, birds, soul effigies, even the breasts of Christ."[23]

The dissonance between the Puritans' verbalized theology and their actualized theology alerts us to how difficult it is to read a culture accurately. Cultures that are in conflict with each other may share more in common than their official self-understandings realize. Many of the things that Puritans abhorred and attacked in others they reintroduced

> in subtle ways here in America. Puritan sermons resonate with theatrical rhetoric even as they denounce the theatre; landscapes and still-lifes surface unexpectedly in the poetry of Benjamin Tompson and Anne Bradstreet; histories and biographies recall the exemplary lives of New England saints with the suspense and adventure of a novel. Although Calvin had declared it idolatrous to represent the deity in corporeal form, some twenty of Edward Taylor's *Preparatory Meditations* explore and linger about the face and body of Christ.[24]

Add these examples to the tombstone icons that include the breasts of Christ, and we sense that the Puritan stridency against images may have arisen from fear that the aesthetic and feminine dimensions of the Divine were alive in their own hearts. Attacking others was a way of suppressing their own urges.

The Internal Contradictions and Complexities of a Church's Culture

Whatever interpretation we may offer of their behavior, the Puritan inconsistency between verbalized and actualized theology is a reminder to us that there may be similar contradictions in us. We need to test if our judgments against different ways of worship and preaching arise from conflicts between what we claim to believe and what in fact we hunger to practice. Indeed, not just the Puritans but the entire long history of the church's oscillation between affirming and denying images is a parable. It invites us to reach for a deeper appreciation of the contradictions that mark our own beliefs and practices. Such awareness can bring the grace of soul, the humility of spirit, and the openness of heart that make us more hospitable to another culture's ways.

When we exercise such hospitality, we will often make surprising discoveries that compel us to reconsider how we have appealed to the church's history and tradition. We will sometimes learn that what we thought had deep theological roots was in fact a matter of practical necessity. For example, the absence of images during the first two centuries of the church's existence was not because Christians were opposed to them. They simply were too poor to afford them.

> The reasons for the nonappearance of Christian art before 200 have nothing to do with principled aversion to art, with otherworldliness or with antimaterialism. The truth is simple and mundane: Christians lacked land and capital. Art required both. As soon as they acquired land and capital, Christians began to experiment with their own distinctive forms of art. But for the earliest segment of their history they remained materially indistinct, an invisible group within the warp and woof of Greco-Roman religions, all of them defined and identified along ethnic lines.[25]

What the early church could afford—not some theological position—shaped its undervisualized culture.

Images as a Strategy for Presenting the Gospel

Once visual images were within its means, the church showed itself open to drawing from the surrounding culture. "The creation of early Christian art seems to have taken place simultaneously and in various places. In every attested example, the scenario involved Christians turning to pagan workshops and exploiting their already existing iconographic repertories."[26] Instead of turning against the dominant culture, the church recognized what a valuable idiom of expression it supplied to the gospel: "The earliest Christians did not set about to uproot the noble trunk of the Greco-Roman artistic past; instead, they grafted their own nascent needs onto this venerable trunk."[27]

Notice how this history of early Christian art modifies our understanding of Christian tradition. When we turn from written texts to material culture, we get an entirely different reading of the interrelationship between the church and culture. We learn that thinking of early Christians as aliens in a hostile world is more the construction of people who live by language and sound rather than by the eye.

The rapidly expanding use of images after 200 C.E. reveals that the boundaries between church and culture were porous, not rigid and solid. Early Christian art "reflects a broad, integrative, and expansive Christianity—one at ease with 'pagan' symbols, one that finds in its Graeco-Roman cultural heritage modes of religious expression that transcend the far narrower confines of Christian texts of the same period."[28]

The amenability of the church to the use of images does not mean that there were no critical standards. After images had established themselves in the life of faith, the church began to struggle with how to relate to the surrounding culture without being drowned by it. Here is Clement of Alexandria writing circa 200 C.E. to establish some principles for deciding whether images are appropriate or inappropriate for Christian use:

> Our seals should be a dove or a fish or a ship running in a fair wind or a musical lyre such as the one Polycrates used or a ship's anchor such as the one Seleucus had engraved on his sealstone. And if someone is fishing he will call to mind the apostle [Peter] and the children [baptizands] drawn up out of the water. We who are forbidden to attach ourselves to idols must not engrave the face of idols [on our rings], or the sword or the bow, since we follow the path of peace, or drinking cups, since we are sober. Many licentious people carry images of their lovers and favorite prostitutes on their rings.[29]

In Clement's quotation it is clear that the church, at this point a relatively minor phenomenon in a much larger world, is still in the process of adapting itself to the dominant culture. But as the church developed and became more prominent, the church went from adapting images for its own use to presenting the case for the gospel through them. The church found itself involved in a full-scale culture war, creating and employing images for the sake of offering an alternative vision to the symbols of the imperial cult of Rome. Images became a strategy for presenting the gospel.

> The fourth century witnessed an unparalleled war of images and it was the strength and energy of the winning images

that determined the outcome. We are more accustomed to narrating events the other way around, describing the winning images as a consequence of the political fortunes of one or another party. But this is to imagine that art is chiefly decoration and illustration, that it merely echoes decisions made in a higher court of activity without taking part in the events of world history. That is not the way things appeared in the fourth century. Constantine had learned in 312 the power of the sign of the cross in his contest with Maxentius at the Battle of the Milvian Bridge. It was Christ who, in a dream, directed him to fashion a Christian symbol on his standards.[30]

Visual Theology: Thinking through Images

The church's use of images was, then, not merely ornamental or supplemental to the use of words. The images were an idiom in their own right for creating and promoting a new culture. The church was working out its theology visually, not just verbally. To the converts of the fourth and fifth century, Christ "was still utterly mysterious, undefinable, changeable, polymorphous. In the disparate images they have left behind they record their struggle to get a grasp on him; the images were their way of thinking out loud on the problem of Christ. Indeed, the images are the thinking process itself."[31]

Most ministers have received rigorous training in the use of words, including profound critical attention to the language of scripture and their tradition. But they have received little or no training in how to understand visual images. This is a major distortion of the Christian tradition that leaves ministers ill-prepared to respond to a contemporary culture in which images are once again one of the primary means by which people think.

If we are ever to understand how "images were [our ancestors'] way of thinking out loud on the problem of Christ," the first step will be to acknowledge the limitations of the ororverbalized culture of theological education. We need to become comfortable in a theological culture that allows for the integrity of the images themselves. That is to say, their interpretation does *not* depend on our assigning a discursive meaning to the image by hooking it up with a biblical text. Instead, we look back and realize that we would not be Christian if our ancestors in the faith had depended on the Bible alone.

The method of proving our interpretation of an image by adducing a text which employs such a meaning has led to a subordination of image to text—as if art could merely reflect a separate intellectual process and not "think on its own." The earliest Christian art, with its happy juxtaposition of pagan, Jewish, and Christian images, its non-narrative, staccato presentation, and its multivalent or ambivalent symbolism definitively challenges the narrower and discursive way of looking at images.[32]

The church's historical use of images as an expression of the gospel filled a gap in the hearts and minds of people that words alone could never reach. It is not outlandish speculation to conclude that Christianity would have disappeared if our ancestors had not mastered the visual elements of the culture in which God called them to give witness. Early Christian artists faced a seemingly insurmountable challenge—translating the gospel into a compelling visual witness in the midst of a culture filled with competing images—and yet they succeeded.

> Scripture had left no account of the physical appearance of Christ, and in any event its claims for Christ far exceeded all visual symbols. How was the artist to deal with Christ's own self-portrait: "Before Abraham was, I am," (Jn 8:58) or "He who has seen me has seen the Father" (Jn 14:9), or "I am the alpha and the omega" (Rev. 1:8)? But, rising to the challenge, painters, sculptors, and mosaic workers invented without inhibition. The narratives of the Gospel they rewrote with freedom to forge images of memorable impact. By representing as many facets of his person as possible they tried to encompass somehow the totality of the unimaginable mystery. Their success spelled the death of the sacred imagery of classical antiquity and the birth of a new, Christian art.[33]

Using the History of Images to Clarify a Church's Worship Practices

The history of how the church honored or denied the use of images illumines our understanding of the interrelationship between culture, preaching, and worship. We can see conflicts and transformations that resonate with our own era's debates about the place of the media in worship and preaching today. In the past the church sometimes welcomed what the larger culture had to offer, and at other times the church drew a boundary between itself and the surrounding culture.

The history of visualization in Christian worship reminds us that the sensorium of the church has oscillated throughout history. No appeal to scripture or tradition has once and for all settled the question of how we are to use our eyes in the worship of God. When we combine this historical fact with our theological principle from chapter 1, "all of us for all of God," we can formulate some guidelines for making decisions about how any particular church can most appropriately engage the eye in worship. We can use a process of discernment that might proceed along the following lines:

- Invite members of the congregation to describe how they use their eyes in worship.
- When are they actively looking, and what do they focus on?
- What is the impact on their participation in worship?
- What are the positive values of using their eyes?
- When do they close their eyes?
- What is the impact on their participation in worship?
- What are the positive values of closing their eyes?
- Let people explain to one another the factors that have shaped their practice.
- Teach members of the congregation the oscillating history of visualization in Christian worship, bringing in books, slides, or PowerPoint presentations that illustrate the history.
- Ask them to identify which parts of that history feel most comfortable to them and which parts are most at odds with their own practice.
- Have them fill out the cultural grid (see chap. 1) under the use of eye, doing it for themselves and for someone in the group who is most different from them.
- Share the differences in the group and talk about what it would take to bring these different cultures of visualization together in worship.
- Design brief liturgical acts that attempt the proposed solutions, and then analyze how they work or do not work.
- On the basis of this entire process, begin to consider how you may want to change the culture of visualization in your current worship practices.

The goal is to place contemporary debates about the use of the eye in worship in a much larger context than individual taste. Will we use film clips? PowerPoint? computerized images? We often ask these questions thinking that they are unique to our age because they involve electronic media that our forebears never dreamed of. The novelty of the media blinds us to finding our deeper links with church history. We fail to consider how our ancestors in the faith struggled over the character of the church's sensorium as it was shaped by their faith and the surrounding culture. Studying the history of conflicts over the use of the eye in worship may lead us to understand how the interrelationship of culture, preaching, and worship has shaped our perspective on the place of the visual in the expression of faith. Freed from identifying our sensorium as the divine mandate of God, we may find ourselves open to new possibilities, and our hearts may be granted a vision of all our forebears—iconoclast and iconophile alike—now beholding God face-to-face and wondering why they never extended more grace to one another on earth.

Working with the congregation on how the eye is used in worship may also enrich our preaching by guiding us into a more profound awareness of what we see and do not see. One of the practices of ancient rhetoric was to instruct speakers in the art of observing a picture or scene and then using that image as a source from which they might draw graphic language. They employed acute visual observation to achieve rhetorical vivacity. Even if our congregational study does not transform the use of the eye in worship, it may vitalize our preaching by making us more attentive to the world God created, the world that, as Genesis 1 tells us again and again, God *saw* was good.

3

EAR

The woman had preached a fine sermon to a group of her peers. The sermon was clear and engaging. She explored the biblical text at a profound level, and her delivery was filled with the Spirit. But during the response session a woman colleague became destructive and biting in her critique of the preacher's sermon. The respondent's petulant tone surprised me and the entire class because she was usually more measured in her judgments. When I asked the respondent the grounds of her uncharacteristic critique, she was silent for a moment. Then she remembered what had happened. Early in the sermon there had been a dramatic story, and the preacher, inflecting the voices of the different characters, had unknowingly echoed the tone that the listener's mother had used to scold her as a child.

Associative Patterns of Sound

The violent reaction to the sermon had nothing to do with the content of the sermon nor its rhetoric nor theology. It was the *sound* of the sermon, the preacher's vocal inflection and all that was awakened by the rise and fall, the beat and pacing of her voice. I call such invocations of meaning that have been awakened by sound "associative patterns." Associative patterns are the constellations of memory and meaning that move not just through words but through the sequences of sound that characterize the aural nature of any culture.

Our class discussion of the incident awakened memories in many of the other students. They recalled preachers who reminded them of angry fathers, bullying coaches, and nagging siblings. The class members did not recall the substance of the sermons but the sound of them and the strong emotive reaction the sound had awakened.

Think of the different sounds you associate with the following:

- a football cheer
- an expression of love by candlelight
- calling to a waiter in a restaurant
- singing happy birthday to a friend
- praying the Lord's Prayer
- an ultimatum delivered by your boss
- a quick greeting on the street
- welcoming people into your home.

All of these are ritual occasions, and we use a different vocal quality for each of them. We did not dream up these sounds on our own. They were taught to us by our culture. We heard them, and we imitated them until they became a part of us. We heard them, and we learned not only what words to say but what tone of voice to use: cheerful, loving, prayerful, excited, self-defending.

Part of what any culture gives us is a world of sound. We operate on the basis of the sonic signals we receive, and we are puzzled if the sound does not match the words. We do not expect "Hello! How are you?" to sound like an ultimatum from the boss. We do not expect a football cheer to sound like the Lord's Prayer. Each has its characteristic inflection, and that inflection awakens associative patterns of memory and meaning.

We learn vocal inflection and its associative patterns not only in our families but also in communities of faith and worship. The way the voice is used to read the Bible aloud during worship varies according to the ecclesial culture of our tradition. My colleague Richard Ward observes that "rules and conventions for effective performances of scripture vary from one community to another."[1] Ward demonstrates how some communities are open to the dramatic performance of biblical texts while others consider a plainer, even-toned delivery essential to honoring the text and God. Vocal inflection is, then, far more than simply a matter of taste. It is an aural manifestation of particular theological understandings about the nature of God's revelation. How God sounds in the ear resonates with how God speaks to the hearts and minds of the congregation.

The Sound of Sermons

What is true of the reading of scripture is even more apparent when we turn to preaching. Ecclesial culture determines how a sermon is to sound. Edmund Steimle, Morris Niedenthal, and Charles Rice ask of preachers the simple but revealing question, "What is the *sound* of a sermon and who planted that sound in your ear?"[2] Although the answer may be a particular preacher, that preacher's sound was most probably shaped by the church culture that nurtured her or him. Different church cultures expect different sounds.

I will never forget a conversation between an American Indian preacher and an African American preacher that I was privileged to hear in a homiletics class. The African American thought that the American Indian had lacked conviction near the end of his sermon because the American Indian spoke the climax in the softest possible voice that could be heard. The American Indian explained in frustration that the softness of his voice was an expression of the depth of his feeling. The African American then realized that he was dealing not with a homiletical absolute, but a cultural difference. His church upbringing had taught him that the climax of a sermon requires a rise in dynamic level, not a softening.

Qualities of sound often symbolize theological understandings: how God is known and revealed, the nature of the church as a receiving and responding community. Drawing on the work of William C. Turner, Jr., Evans Crawford terms the sound of African American preaching "homiletical musicality," meaning "the way in which the preacher uses timing, pauses, inflection, pace, and the other musical qualities of speech to engage all that the listener is in the act of proclamation. This musicality represents something much deeper than method. It is an expression of the holy God working through the preacher and the community, and it requires a rigorous and authentic spirituality on the part of both preacher and congregation."[3]

The sound of the sermon is so important to the culture of many African American churches that there is sometimes a bias against university training because it has "compromised the desirable oral performance abilities of some preachers, even though well-educated preachers are highly prized as pastors."[4] This bias is *not* a form of anti-intellectualism. It is rather an affirmation of the highly sophisticated use of sound as a means of communication and religious expression. "It is the preacher's task and duty to charge the preaching environment with dynamic energies and in so doing to induce the congregation to focus oral and aural mechanisms on the content and structure of the sermon performance."[5]

Who planted the sound of preaching in your ear? You may remember a particular preacher, but that preacher would not have survived long in the pulpit unless his or her voice fell within the acceptable range of the culture's sonic values.

In many cases, however, the sound of preaching that is acceptable to a church becomes a tangled issue, especially for women who preach in a sexist culture. When women receive a call to become ordained clergy, they often struggle to achieve a sound in their preaching that is acceptable to the church and congruent with the distinctive identity God has given them. As Lee McGee has documented through her research, women possess in their depths the memory of women's voices that shaped their spiritual life, but those memories are often suppressed by the culture of both church and society, so that they need to be reclaimed through a "voice retrieval process."[6]

Although the resistance to women in positions of religious authority has many complex roots, at least one of those roots is an ecclesial culture that has planted in the ears of men and women a particular sound for preaching and liturgical leadership. Sometimes in my travels as I preach, elderly women will say to me, "It is so nice to hear a man's deep voice when you preach."

Such statements can be explicated at many levels, including the physiological fact that as we age it becomes more difficult to hear higher pitches. The elderly women are simply grateful to hear more of what is said. Their aural world is shrinking, and they hunger to feel again that fuller inclusion in the community that once was theirs when their hearing was keener.

But the comments also reflect a cultural bias: These are elderly women who when they were children grew up with a sound of preaching that was in almost all cases masculine. Their response arises from what their childhood culture taught them, the sound of preaching it planted in their ears.

The Sound of Silence

What is true of sound is equally true of silence. We can think of silence as a particular species of sound, as when we "hear" a pause in someone's speech or a rest in a piece of music or when we are "struck" by the silence of some vast, uninhabited space. Silence is not a neutral aural state for hearing persons.

Jane Vennard, who has worked extensively in the field of spiritual direction, has encountered a range of negative responses to the use of silence in retreats. Sometimes the silence is threatening, because we in America live in a culture of perpetual sound.

> Our homes may be filled with the whining of kitchen appliances, the clanking of exercise equipment, and the beeping of computers. People carry their own boom boxes. Cars play stereos at top volume. Neighborhoods are filled with power lawn mowers, leaf blowers, and snow blowers. City streets sport garbage trucks, jackhammers, and backfiring buses. Whistles blow, sirens shriek, horns honk, and helicopters fly overhead. Stores play music continually, people talk through movies and concerts, and cell phones ring in church.[7]

To move out of this sonic world into silence can represent a cultural shift that is as disorienting as arrival in a foreign country where you know neither the language nor the customs.

To many Americans the absence of sound may seem like the disappearance of the world, the evaporation of reality. But to other cultures silence is an essential part of successful communication. Eunjoo Kim explains that "in contemporary Asian communication, silence is regarded as an effective communication form. It does not mean an embarrassing moment that occurs by a sudden break in the flow of words, but a comfortable tranquility that occurs when the speaker and the hearer identify so fully that they need no words to confirm their rapport."[8]

Compare the "comfortable tranquility" of silence in Asian communication to the American compulsion to fill the air with sound at all times, including the playing of Muzak in elevators and over the telephone while you are on hold. I have been told by businesspeople that music or recorded promotional chatter is essential to keeping customers on the line. Callers will hang up before they will wait through silence.

Or consider the way liturgists and preachers in most American services feel they must never allow more than a few brief seconds for silent prayer or a sermonic pause. Our homiletical and liturgical practices continue the sonic saturation of the surrounding culture. There are some exceptions to this, most notably in African American preaching, which uses the pause "as a metaphor of spiritual formation, as an acknowledgement by preachers that they must not cram the air so full of their words that they obscure the vast and silent mystery from which true speech arises."[9]

The African American's use of the homiletical pause is similar to the Asian writer or speaker who "leaves space, pausing for some time between sentences or words, because verbalized images alone are incomplete for creative communication. Here, space or timing does not simply designate a meaningless void or state of naught but rather connotes a 'reservoir of meanings' that provides the listeners or the readers with a reflective moment. It is a sort of aesthetic experience in communication shared by Asians."[10]

Many pastors from white Protestant American congregations have told me over the years that their attempts to use more silence in worship and preaching have met resistance. Sometimes the resistance represents more than the simple discomfort of a people accustomed to always having sound in the air. It may also arise from painful memories. In a culture where sound is the norm, silence is often used to punish, manipulate, or shun individuals. By refusing to speak to someone, we cut that person out of our world. Silence becomes a hostile act, a form of violence that disrupts relationships. "'When my wife is angry with me, she gives me "the silent treatment." I don't know what I have done, and I feel uneasy and on edge,' one man reported. A young woman shared that her father used to clam up, not speak during dinner, not wish her good night. Her father's silence frightened her because it was usually followed by an explosion of anger."[11]

In other cases, particularly for women and marginalized peoples, silence may be an enforced state. The dominant powers refuse to give them voice in the public arena. Therefore, to break the enforced silence "is an expression that reacts to oppressive forces in order to find freedom, be it for oneself or for others with whom a person identifies."[12]

Varied Functions of Speech and Silence

Silence and speech, depending on our culture, can function in radically different ways for people of faith. Barbara Brown Taylor observes that we sometimes need silence to correct the verbosity of our religious life. We speak constantly without giving God a chance, because "staying preoccupied with our own words seems a safer bet than opening ourselves up either to God's silence or God's speech, both of which have the power to undo us."[13]

Taylor's insight finds its reverse image in Nelle Morton's equally compelling claim: "I want to posit the possibility that there is a word, that there are so many words, awaiting woman speech. And perhaps there is a word that has not yet come to sound—a word that once we begin to speak will round out and create deeper experience for us and put us in touch with sources of power, energy of which we are just beginning to become aware."[14]

Do we need silence or speech to encounter the divine "power"? (Taylor and Morton both use the same word.) The traditional Protestant answer is that we need speech, or more precisely, we need to hear a word from the Lord. Luther, drawing on Paul's statement that "faith comes from what is heard" (Rom. 10:17), puts the matter as forcefully as anyone ever has:

> God no longer requires the feet or the hands or any other member: He requires only the ears...For if you ask a Christian what the work is by which he becomes worthy of the name "Christian," he will be able to give absolutely no other answer than that it is the hearing of the Word of God, that is, faith. Therefore the ears alone are the organs of a Christian man, for he is justified and declared to be a Christian, not because of the works of any members but because of faith.[15]

These words made perfect sense for Luther, who was writing in an overvisualized, ecclesial culture (see chap. 2). But nowadays the answer to our question—Do we need silence or speech to encounter the divine power?—is much more complex. It depends on our cultural context, our position in society, and all the associations that silence and speech carry in our hearts. Preachers and liturgists oblivious to these matters may confuse their own cultural predilections with theological absolutes, making judgments about speech or silence that are not shared by the culture of the congregation.

The Sound of Sense

So far I have dealt exclusively with sound and silence. I have said nothing about rhetorical strategy, biblical interpretation, or theological content. We will consider these matters in chapter 4, but I have eschewed them here in order to emphasize the different ways that sound and silence function in different cultures. The ear may bypass language and respond to the sound of the voice rather than the meaning of the words. In the opening story of this chapter the listener reacted not to the preacher's eloquent message, but to the preacher's vocal inflection that reminded the listener of her mother scolding her as a little girl.

If we leap too quickly to text and to words, we may subvert the work of cultural analysis by avoiding sound and the associative patterns that it awakens. As a preacher and a poet, I love words, but words have their limits. I have come to realize that sound often determines meaning as much, if not more, than language alone. Robert Frost understood this:

> Words in themselves do not convey meaning...[L]et us take
> the example of two people who are talking on the other side
> of a closed door, whose voices can be heard but whose words
> cannot be distinguished. Even though the words do not carry,
> the sound of them does, and the listener can catch the mean-
> ing of the conversation...[T]he sense of every meaning has a
> particular sound...[T]he sound of sense existed before
> words.[16]

The "sound of sense" may have been even more self-evident to
ancient worshipers because for them there was not such a sharp
distinction between speech and music as there is for us.

> Public utterance was closer to chanting than speaking. An-
> cient Greek poetry, for example, was probably chanted,
> moving between the ground note of the poem and a note
> above it, probably a fourth or a fifth. This is what the Greeks
> called "music." First-century synagogue worship migrated
> between speech and song. By contrast, first-century Chris-
> tian worship "song" was probably closer to a ring-shout than
> to a cathedral choir.[17]

The Sound of Music

Culture determines our response to music every bit as much as it
shapes our understanding of the vocal inflection of speech. Contrary
to popular wisdom, music is not a universal language. For example,
the minor keys of Western music are generally taken to be an
expression of sadness and lament, but quite often they are used to
awaken energy and celebration in Hebraic music.[18] The same musical
key carries different associative patterns according to the culture in
which we are raised. The meaning of the sound is a function of our
conditioning.

Even the exact same melody may awaken different associative
patterns. Consider, for example, the musical setting "Austria," included
in many standard hymnals to accompany John Newton's hymn text,
"Glorious Things of Thee Are Spoken." Long before I sang it as a
hymn in church, I knew the tune from sitting in my father's lap and
listening to it on 78 rpm records as the movement from a string quartet
that Franz Joseph Haydn composed in 1797. Haydn himself adapted
it from a Croatian folk song. Later in my childhood I would sing the
tune in church while standing next to my mother. The beauty of the
melody and my personal associative patterns of its relationship to
both my father and mother made it precious to me.

"Glorious Things of Thee Are Spoken" was chosen to open a graduation ceremony in which Elie Weisel, the famous Holocaust survivor and theologian, received an honorary doctorate. It happens that the tune was also the setting for the national anthem of the Third Reich, "Deutschland, Deutschland über Alles." The use of it at the graduation ceremony was innocent of any malice. Those who chose it had no knowledge of the tune's associations with the Nazis. But imagine how terrifying it was to Weisel to hear the organ introduce that tune! His associative patterns were utterly different from mine. The tune evoked not loving parents, but the unspeakable terror of genocide.

We learn sound in a particular context that feeds us with memories and meanings. "The language and dialect of music are many. They vary from culture to culture, from epoch to epoch within the same culture and even within a single epoch and culture."[19] A culture's judgments about sound are as powerful as its strictures about the use of the eye. Anyone doubting this has only to step into the debate about what kind of music is appropriate in worship!

As someone who creates new hymn texts and works with many composers writing in different musical idioms, I have personally experienced how difficult it is to stretch the range of a culture's sonic idiom. For example, many years ago I wrote a hymn text on one of the exorcism stories from the gospels. Although the meter was 8-7-8-7 doubled, one of the more frequent meters of English language hymnody, when I finished the first stanza, I already sensed that I was writing language that would require a different musical sound from the standard settings found in hymn books.

> "Silence! Frenzied, unclean spirit,"
> cried God's healing, holy One.
> "Cease your ranting! Flesh can't bear it
> Flee as night before the sun."
> At Christ's voice the demon trembled,
> from its victim madly rushed,
> while the crowd that was assembled
> stood in wonder, stunned and hushed.[20]

The composer, Carol Doran, provided a musical setting that was truly exorcising: an insistent repeated beat that hammers the demonic spirit out of the soul. When we presented this new hymn at a national conference, an older clergyman came up and complained that it "did not sound like a hymn," while a teenager said, "I loved that hymn the best of all you did." Each responded out of the sonic culture in which he had been raised.

Through their diametrically different responses I was experiencing a major shift in musical culture that is part of a much larger historical and cultural process. Brian Wren conveniently compresses these transitions into three acute observations: "In Western music, melody was dominant during the era of plainsong. Later, harmony came to prominence. In contemporary music, rhythm takes center stage."[21] The older priest was the product of a culture that relishes melody and harmony, and the teenager was the product of a culture that exults in strong, percussive rhythm. These different sonic cultures are now frequently colliding in churches of every tradition. They result in arguments about the relative merits of pipe organs, electric organs, synthesizers, SATB choirs, folk song, gospel rock, praise choruses, hymns, new age music, and so forth. If people start only from the limits of their own sonic culture, assuming it is normative, then it becomes impossible for them to consider why a different sonic culture means so much to another group. Furthermore, they may miss the call of the Spirit to expand their sonic culture as a way of grasping more fully the multiplicity of ways in which faith is made musically manifest.

The Sonic Culture of the Early Church

We are not the first people to debate the place of music in the church. The history of the use of the ear in worship is every bit as conflicted as the use of the eye! Tensions over music have been with us from the moment the gospel spread around the Mediterranean basin. The church encountered pagan cultures that employed music to induce ecstasy and to engage people's emotions. The rhapsodic power of music made it suspect to philosophers, including Plato, whose love-hate relationship to the art had a profound impact on the church.

> On the one hand, [Plato] embraced the use of music as one of the cornerstones in shaping human character; on the other, he feared its power, and his suspicion led him to establish elaborate guidelines severely to circumscribe its influence. The Christian church inherited this tension, and it characterized its relationship to music for at least the first one and one-half millennia of its existence.[22]

The emotional character of pagan music amplified the church's ambiguity about its use in worship. The church could not wholeheartedly embrace an art closely associated with its opponents, and yet the church fathers recognized music as an effective medium of corporate prayer. Saint Augustine was among the many early

Christian thinkers who attempted to disentangle music from its pagan associations.

> We must not shun music because of the superstition of the heathen, if we are able to snatch from it anything useful for the understanding of the Holy Scriptures; and we need not be involved with their theatrical frivolities, if we consider some point concerning citharas and other instruments which might be of aid in comprehending spiritual things.[23]

As Christian theology interpreted its beliefs in light of Greek philosophy, the thought of Pythagoras and Plato became especially significant to its theological understanding of music. Their canons of musical taste helped to shape the sonic culture of Western worship. Drawing from the Greeks' ideas, the church came to understand music as a discipline that forms human character by revealing something of the nature of God and the world that God has created. As early as the beginning of the third century of our era, Hippolytus writes:

> Now Pythagoras, in his investigation of nature, combined astronomy, geometry, music [and arithmetic]. He thus declared that God is a monad; and, thoroughly schooled in the properties of number, he said that the world sings *(melodein)* and is made up of harmony...The world, he said, is like a musical harmony, and that this is why the sun makes its circuit in accordance with harmony.[24]

Because God created the world to be harmonious, it followed that human beings were most aligned with the divine intention when they themselves were harmonious. Harmonious music expressed the harmonious character of a godly life.

> The Lord made man [sic] a beautiful breathing instrument after his own image; certainly he is himself an all harmonious instrument of God, well tuned and holy, the transcendental wisdom, the heavenly Word...This is the New Song, the shining manifestation among us now of the Word, who was in the beginning and before the beginning.[25]

Claiming an ethical dimension to music empowered the church to become hospitable to its use. The church justified its musical practices through an appeal to allegorical, symbolic, and magical meanings.[26]

The church assembled over time a particular understanding of what kind of sound the ear should receive in worship. Not just any sound would be let into the liturgy. For if the church were open to every kind of sound, its worship would lose its distinctively Christian character. The early and patristic church concluded that the appropriate qualities of music for worship were

- nobility
- majesty
- the ability to calm the soul

By favoring these qualities, the church limited the emotional range of music, rejecting those excesses that it associated with paganism. Its tonal palette and the spiritual values evoked by a particular species of sound helped the church to establish a culture that was distinctive from the surrounding world.

We do not know if all churches accepted these standards of musical judgment. But, as we will discover in chapter 4, there is evidence that churches were not of one mind about what was to be considered appropriate gesture and movement, so it is not unreasonable to speculate that there was a similar variety of musical styles. For there were Christians who, following a service of worship, gladly gave themselves to the pleasures of what was considered by the church fathers to be "godless" music. Clement of Alexandria (circa 150–215 C.E.) tells us about them:

> After reverently attending to the discourse about God, they left what they had heard within, while outside they amuse themselves with godless things, with the plucking of strings *(kroumaton)* and the erotic wailing of the aulos, defiling themselves with dancing *(krotou),* drunkenness and every sort of trash. Those who sing thus and sing in response are those who hymned immortality before, but sing finally, wicked and wickedly, that vicious recantation: "Let us eat and drink, for tomorrow we die."[27]

Clement's disgust with believers indulging in pagan song continued as a theme for the next two centuries, so that "there is hardly a major church father from the fourth century who does not inveigh against pagan musical practice in the strongest language."[28]

The early church fathers who favored emotional restraint in music appealed to a metaphor drawn from Greek philosophy: Music is an expression of the harmony of the spheres, of just proportion, of the beauty and balance of creation, of the mathematical perfection of God's work. It would be difficult to exaggerate the grip of this metaphor on Christian thinking about music. The harmony of the spheres as a metaphor justifying the use of music in worship returns again and again throughout the history of the church. It is much loved and often invoked by church composers, preachers, and liturgists. From age to age the harmony of the spheres reinforced the bias of the church against what it considered the excesses of pagan music.

Historic Transformation of the Church's Sonic Culture

With the rise of humanism, both inside and outside the church, there was increased attention to the individual and to human emotion, and this transformed the standards for music in church. Instruments, for example, which had been banned because of their pagan associations and because they made music without words, became very popular in church. A print from circa 1590 shows a band of wind instrumentalists, including horn, trombone, and oboe players, gathered at the steps to a high altar while the celebrants are raising their hands in prayer.[29]

Humanism brought another reversal in the thought and practice of the church's music: The emotional appeal of music that the early church had rejected as unchristian now became a valued quality in light of the new focus on the human individual.

To feel how dramatic this shift in the musical culture of the church was, consider the contrast between one of the greatest and most beloved of all Latin hymns, the *Te Deum*, which "surely dates at least to the fourth century,"[30] and one of the most beloved hymns of evangelical Protestantism in the United States, "How Great Thou Art."[31] The latter hymn can be found in several denominational hymnals.[32] First I will analyze the texts; then I will turn to musical considerations. Here is the *Te Deum*:

> You are God: we praise you;
> You are the Lord: we acclaim you;
> You are the eternal Father:
> All creation worships you.
> To you all angels, all the powers of heaven,
> Cherubim and Searphim, sing in endless praise:
> Holy, holy, holy Lord, God of power and might,
> heaven and earth are full of your glory.
> The glorious company of apostles praise you.
> The noble fellowship of prophets praise you.
> The white-robed army of martyrs praise you.
> Throughout the world the holy Church acclaims you;
> Father, of majesty unbounded,

your true and only Son, worthy of all worship,
and the Holy Spirit, advocate and guide.
You, Christ, are the king of glory,
the eternal Son of the Father.
When you became man to set us free
you did not shun the Virgin's womb.
You overcame the sting of death
and opened the kingdom of heaven to all believers.
You are seated at God's right hand in glory.
We believe that you will come and be our judge.
Come then, Lord, and help your people,
bought with the price of your own blood,
and bring us with your saints
to glory everlasting.[33]

Both hymns are about the transcendent, mighty, creating, redeeming God, but how different the way they give expression to this belief!

The *Te Deum* uses the first person plural, "We," while "How Great Thou Art" uses the first person singular, "I." The *Te Deum* ascribes praise, acclamation, and worship to God through the entire creation and the faithful witnesses of history: "angels," "powers of heaven," "Cherubim and Seraphim," the "company of apostles," the "fellowship of martyrs," and the "army of martyrs." "How Great Thou Art" leaves us with a solitary self throughout. Instead of the vast array of witnesses to God invoked by the *Te Deum*, "How Great Thou Art" employs a single, solitary "I" that looks at the stars and wanders through the woods and reflects on Christ's atonement.

This constant stress on "I" results in a constricted understanding of salvation and a presumption of worthiness: In the final stanza the "I" does not ask to be mercifully received at death but presumes that Christ has no choice. The *Te Deum* eschews human presumption. It respects the freedom of Christ to decide what ought to happen to us: "We believe that you will come and be our judge." The *Te Deum* concludes not with self-centered security, but with a prayer for the community: "Come then, Lord, and help your people."

If an individual loses faith or goes through a time of doubt, "How Great Thou Art" leaves that person to struggle alone in reestablishing a relationship to God. But the *Te Deum* reminds the person of the vast historical and cosmic company that are praising God no matter what the state of the individual soul. The *Te Deum* keeps the individual connected to a web of worship and faith greater than the self so that the self is much less at the mercy of its unique psychological dynamics.

How Sonic Culture May Override Verbal Function

The preceding analytical comparison between the *Te Deum* and "How Great Thou Art" is based entirely on the texts. If we apply our principle that sound often supersedes language, the two poems, when they are sung, may function in ways that are far different from their literal content. For example, if we have been raised in an American evangelical Protestant church, in which "How Great Thou Art" is one of the most frequently sung and beloved hymns, it may carry associations that give it the very qualities its language lacks. When we hear it, we may recall our family and friends singing it around us while we grew up and we may feel connected to their corporate witness. We may remember when we accepted Christ with a number of other people and feel again their faith and joy as well as ours. We may remember when it was sung at a wedding or a funeral, and it may help us reclaim vital connections to others. Or perhaps the cumulative power of all these memories will make the hymn a vessel of the Spirit that is empowering us to do justice and show compassion in the larger community.

In short, we cannot make judgments about such pieces purely on the basis of how they appear on a sheet of paper. There is a culture of sound whose attendant webs of meaning may extend far beyond what is on the page. If we try to settle debates about such matters merely on the basis of what is there on the printed page, we will be bypassing the complex source of people's passions.

Attentiveness to the culture of sound and how a piece may function does not preclude educating a congregation to the development and transformation of the church's culture over time. Without such education and without actually singing a wide range of music, churches run the risk of constricting the human heart so that people lack the capacity to think critically about what they sing. They will no longer practice the wisdom of Paul: "I will sing praise with the spirit, but I will sing praise with the mind also" (1 Cor. 14:15).

The History of the Ear in Worship Clarifies a Church's Sonic Culture

Quentin Faulkner believes that music has now "become a theological orphan. In fact, no important theological movement, either in the nineteenth or twentieth century, has concerned itself in any profound way with the significance of harmony, order, or beauty in Christian life or cult."[34] I take exception to the sweeping nature of this last statement when I think of Hans Urs von Balthasar's theological work on beauty. Nevertheless, Faulkner is naming a genuine weakness in most of our debates about music in worship. Many churches lack theological and artistic standards that can help them make informed musical decisions. Although worship can effectively employ a wide range of music, services often end up a mishmash of selections so that the liturgy is a diffuse event rather than a vessel of corporate prayer.

Here is a process to help churches clarify their sonic culture and formulate musical and artistic standards that are appropriate to their liturgical life. There are three primary steps:

- Introduce people to the concept of a sonic culture. Have them recall the particular sounds with which they grew up: a parent's voice, an athletic cheer, a boss on the phone, the Lord's Prayer, sermons, concerts, music they play and sing, music they associate with church. Consider as well the different ways they respond to silence.

- Have congregation members fill out the exercise sheet on page 59. It is designed to help them identify the sonic culture that they bring to church and that they expect to experience in worship.

- Outline a theological framework for making musical/liturgical judgments.

In workshops, I model the third step by outlining my own theological framework. I have found that as long as I remain open to their particular needs, people appreciate seeing a pattern for thinking about music and worship. I am asking them to do something that most of them have never done before, and, therefore, it is helpful to see how someone else has gone about the task.

Participants often begin with the assumption that all the others bear in their heads the same culture that they do. But our discussion nearly always reveals that is not the case. This is as true for sound as it is for the other dimensions of the sensorium.

On the next page is the exercise sheet that I use with worship and music committees or with gatherings of a cross-section of the congregation.

I usually find the results of this exercise to be complex. There are often strong convergences—for example, Christmas carols and Easter hymns—and strong divergences, especially between those who love chorales and those who love Christian rock. If, however, the group enters the exercise with a genuine commitment to hearing the sources of their varied responses, it often is the start of coming to some mutual understanding. People begin a process of cross-cultural communication, which in its deeper theological dimensions represents the work of reconciliation that has been entrusted to us by God (2 Cor. 5:18–21).

Identifying the Sonic Culture I Bring to Worship

Rationale:

The memories and customs that people bring from their past often have a controlling influence over what they expect in church. These memories, especially musical memories, run deep in the blood, and they can exercise a hidden power over people's responses to worship, because they have never been brought to awareness. This exercise is designed to help us become aware of our own deep memories and to see how they compare with the memories of others in our church.

Process:

Step 1. List your three favorite pieces of music for worship. They can include any form and style of music, from what the congregation sings to what a choir or soloist sings or plays. The pieces you choose should be the ones that thrill your heart, that lift you into a state of prayer, that give you a sense of the presence of the Spirit, that strengthen your faith, that bring a lump to the throat or tears to the eyes.

_____

_____

_____

Step 2. For each piece, identify, if possible, how and where your learned it and/or any particular memory or association that the piece has for you.

_____

_____

_____

Step 3. Now step outside of your personal experiences and take the role of one who is to plan and lead worship for *the whole congregation.* What do you see as strengths in the pieces you have identified? Weaknesses?

_____

_____

_____

Step 4. Compare your selections, associations, and evaluations with those of two other people from the congregation. How are they similar? How are they different? Do you judge them to be compatible or in conflict? Why?

Although I use the exercise to begin a long-term conversation among the members of the congregation, participants find it helpful when I share the theological principles I have been developing for making musical/liturgical decisions. The issue is not whether or not they share my sonic culture. Rather, the issue is learning to think about the impact of a culture of sound and its implications for our worship. What follows is the kind of thinking out loud that I do before the group.

Principle One: The Complete Word Has the Nature of Song

Music brings the word of God to a fullness of expression never achieved by words alone. I think, for example, of a woman I met during a worship and music conference. In conversation she listened far more than she spoke, yet her face revealed that she was absorbing and processing everything she heard. When she sang a solo in a service, the richness of soul that was hinted by her expressive face became manifest as sound. Making music transfigured her whole being. A stream of melody poured out of her, and the loveliness of the sound opened the congregation to the Spirit that prays for us "with sighs too deep for words" (Rom. 8:26).

In my theology, those "sighs too deep for words" are part of God's Word. They are God's speaking to us in ways that move beyond the limits of human speech. They complete the word of God as a kiss completes the word *love,* as a dance of delight completes the word *joy,* as a look of awe completes the word *wonder.* Love, joy, wonder— are all splendid words, but saying them is not enough. The realities they name overflow the banks of language, and that is what music at its best does in worship. It is part of the overflowing of the divine Word that is greater than words.

I was the preacher for the service, but I had no illusion that I was the only one proclaiming the Word and giving witness to Christ and the Spirit. How thankful I was for that woman's song! The music carried the congregation beyond my broken articulations as a preacher to the sacred source from whom song and sermon alike arose. I experienced the truth of Joseph Gelineau's observation that

> the word which is merely spoken is a somewhat incomplete
> form of human language. It suffices for ordinary utilitarian
> communications. But as soon as the word becomes charged
> with emotion, as soon as it is filled with power, as soon as it
> tends to identify itself with the content of its message—...it

has to signify the sacredness of actions being performed—
then it calls imperatively...for a musical form...The complete word, the fully developed word, has the nature of song.[35]

Because the "complete word" possesses "the nature of song," the
proclamation of the Word is incomplete and distorted without song.
Song, whatever its particular cultural expression, is not something
added to the Word simply to make the proclamation more appealing.
Sacred song is as much a part of the proclamation of the Word and
the pastoral care of the church as are preaching, prayer, and ritual
action.

Principle Two: Ambivalence about Music in Worship Is Part of Our Christian Inheritance

Our debates about music in worship too often ignore the historical
and theological roots of the conflict. These roots go much deeper
than individual personalities and tastes. We live in a society that has
a short-term historical memory—this morning's CNN lead story may
not survive till the evening news—and yet we still are influenced by
the past more than we realize. The biases of our ancestors leave a
genetic stamp on our thought through their bequests of language,
practice, attitude, and belief. We inherit culturally shaped forms of
thought without any critical awareness of them, and this is as true
about church music as it is about any other arena of the church's
theology and ministry.

The church has inherited something of Paul's nervousness about
music. We detect his wariness in his assertion to the Corinthians, "I
will sing praise with the spirit, but I will sing praise with the mind
also" (1 Cor. 14:15). Paul makes this remark while insisting on the
need for clarity and comprehensibility in worship, and he seems eager
that those values be as prominent when we sing as when we speak.
An earlier aside about "lifeless instruments that produce sound, such
as the flute or the harp" (1 Cor. 14:7) and his famous statement that
not to have love is to be "a noisy gong or a clanging cymbal" (1 Cor.
13:1) suggest that Paul was wary of music and its power. Gongs and
cymbals were frequently employed in pagan worship, so Paul's
ambivalence about music arises in part from the need to help
Christians establish an identity that is distinctive from the surrounding
culture.

Ambivalence about the use of music in worship continued to be
a theme in the writing of Christian thinkers for the next four centuries.
No one is more articulate about it than Augustine, who in his *Confessions*

moves back and forth between the delight he takes in music and his fear that music will lead him away from God's Word:

> I vacillate between the peril of pleasure and the value of the experience, and I am led more—while advocating no irrevocable position—to endorse the custom of singing in church so that by the pleasure of hearing the weaker soul might be elevated to an attitude of devotion. Yet when it happens to me that the song moves me more than the thing which is sung, I confess that I have sinned blamefully and then prefer not to hear the singer.[36]

The early centuries of Christianity found many congregations as ambivalent as Paul and Augustine about the use of music in worship. Believers recognized the power of music to grip people's hearts and minds, but they continued to be wary of the pagan associations of music. They were suspicious that the emotional and ritual excesses of music that characterized the cultic assemblies of other beliefs might corrode Christian worship. Tatian, writing circa 160 C.E., disparages what he considers to be musical immorality: "I do not wish to gape at many singers nor do I care to look benignly upon a man who is nodding and motioning in an unnatural way."[37]

It is not wild speculation to compare the early fears of pagan influence to contemporary resistance to new forms of music in our congregations. Like us, those early Christians initially lacked a theology of music that would allow them to engage the sonic cultures that surrounded them, but the constant pressure of the surrounding environment made it impossible to avoid the issue. And so the church began to draw from the philosophers of ancient Greece to formulate an understanding of music that they considered coherent with their belief. This intellectual work belonged to the much larger theological project of integrating the gospel with the thought forms that the church encountered as it spread around the Mediterranean basin.

The conversation between faith and philosophy, between ecclesial and pagan cultures, gave birth to principles that guided the musical practices of the church at worship. The principles, reflecting a heavy debt to the thought of Pythagoras and Plato, included:[38]

- Music is a science featuring arithmetical relationships.
- Music can influence behavior and hence has a moral dimension.
- Interpreting music theologically and metaphysically leads to understanding it through allegory, symbolism, and magic.

These principles were used to guard against the excesses of music. Many churches favored music of a limited emotional range that did not awaken sensuality. The hope was that music would attune the congregation to the harmony of the heavens, an idea that finds expression again and again through the history of Christian ideas about music.

Principle Three: The Church's Theology of Music Has Fragmented

Like all systems of thought, the theology of music that many churches developed through conversation with Greek philosophy did not last forever. As the gospel spread into Europe and encountered new cultures, the theological/musical ideals that originated among churches in the Mediterranean basin began to crumble. They broke up under the stress of many forces, including

- the turn toward individualistic piety
- the objectification of reality that characterized the scientific revolution and the enlightenment
- the rise of romanticism, with its stress on personal experience and depth of affective expression[39]
- the breakdown of accepted authority through the modern era
- the increasing awareness of cultural differences and the role culture plays in shaping our values, our understandings of race and gender, and our theologies
- the impact of mass media and multimedia in creating segmented audiences that are attuned to particular musical idioms

These factors eroded the integration of Christian theology and classical thought, and with the demise of that synthesis came the collapse of the church's coherent philosophy of music in worship.[40] The church no longer possesses a common conceptual framework for understanding the place of music in the life of faith. Musicians, pastors, and worship committees feel the burden of the collapsed system of meanings, values, and understandings.

Music is especially liable to bearing the burden of this fragmentation because of the associative patterns that music carries in people's memories. When these patterns are threatened, people respond out of the depths of who they are. They refuse to sing new hymns or new words to familiar musical settings or to try new forms of congregational song. They balk at purchasing new hymnals or permitting new instruments and sounds into their services.

Something greater than nostalgia or pigheadedness is at work in these reactions. People are fighting to survive as practicing believers. In my experience, however, when liturgical leaders address the deeper spiritual and theological anxieties that feed resistance to change, I find an increasing willingness to consider what is new. We might compare this situation to the difference between the writer of Psalm 137 and the postexilic sections of Isaiah. The psalmist, bereft of Jerusalem and the temple, mourns "How could we sing the LORD's song in a foreign land?" (Ps. 137:4), while Isaiah declares, "Sing to the LORD a new song, his praise from the end of the earth!" (Isa. 42:10). Isaiah addresses the deeper spiritual and theological anxieties by insisting that God is doing a "new thing" (Isa. 43:19), and God's new action requires a new song, not simply one of the remembered songs of the past.

Principle Four: Fragmentation May Provide Openings for the Spirit

Periods of fragmentation have often been the prelude to receiving the Spirit in new ways and to revitalizing the religious imagination of the community of faith. As we have just noted, the destruction of the temple and the exile to Babylon gave rise to a more expansive vision of God in the theology of Isaiah. In a similar manner, John, the writer of Revelation, exiled to the island of Patmos and suffering the loss of his community of faith, interwove his visionary work with hymns and anthems to proclaim that the songful praise of God would endure and continue long after the Roman Empire had collapsed. Perhaps God is calling us to use our current fragmentation to rethink the theological meaning of music in the same spirit of creativity as Isaiah, Revelation, and the Patristic Church. For even though there has been in recent times a great deal of activity in church music, it "has given rise to scant theological reflection as to its purpose."[41]

We cannot reassemble the syntheses of the past, but we can start with church music as we know it at its best. Then we can ask what are the theological and pastoral dynamics that make such music a vessel of the Spirit, an expression of prayer, an opening to the holy. Our method, like that of much contemporary theology, will be grounded in the actuality of our experience, in this case the experience of singing and playing and listening.

As an example of this method of reflection on ecclesial sonic culture, I return to the woman who poured out her soul in song at the music and worship conference. Some time after the conference, she phoned me long distance to ask if I would write a hymn text to honor her church's organist and choirmaster. She acknowledged him to be not only a splendid musician but a person with one of the most precious of all gifts: the ability to draw forth the gifts of others. He had encouraged the woman to sing, as he had scores of others. When I asked if there were to be a particular theme for the hymn, she informed me that the choir director's favorite parable was the story of the ten talents (Mt. 25:14–30). I subsequently wrote the hymn, "For God Risk Everything." I realize now what I did not realize while I was creating the piece: The poem identifies yet more principles for formulating a contemporary philosophy of church music.

I will use the poem in order to model the theological/cultural method that I am urging on musicians, pastors, and worship committees: Draw from your own practice in order to identify the principles that are shaping your ecclesial sonic culture.

> For God risk everything
> since everything we own,
> our laughter, tears, the songs we sing,
> our breath, our flesh and bone,
> are no more ours to keep
> than wind that rushes by
> or dreams that flicker in our sleep
> or clouds that fade to sky.[42]

Writing such a hymn flows not simply from my own inner world. It arises out of the memory of all the churches that are experiencing fragmentation and conflict. Their brokenness, like the brokenness known to Isaiah and to John on the island of Patmos, creates an opening for new visions. Fragmentation encourages me to find a fresh idiom to give witness to God, who provides the only hope for the enduring reconciliation of conflicting cultures.

Principle Five: Singing Manifests Our Creaturehood

No matter what our ecclesial sonic culture, singing is a risk.

- What sound will issue from our mouths?
- Will we be in tune?
- Will our voice blend with others?
- Will it crack and scratch the air?

We will never know unless we take a breath and open our mouths and let the sound out. Singing is a physiological action that reminds us of the truth that shines through the opening chapters of Genesis: We are earthen creatures (*Adam* = from the earth) into whom our Creator has breathed breath. While we may live with the illusions that success and wealth afford us, the fact remains that our physical being is "no more ours to keep/than wind that rushes by/or dreams that flicker in our sleep/or clouds that fade to sky."

Singing as an expression of faith and praise manifests our creaturehood. It is an action that requires us to use the materiality of who we are in the praise of the One who has formed us. We do not just think theological thoughts about creation, we actualize them as we fill our lungs with air and return our breath through the larynx and against the soft and hard structures of the mouth into the atmosphere. Although different cultures teach people to sing in different ways, no culture can override the physical reality of the human body. We cannot sing without breath passing over vocal chords. Hence, the production of sound in the praise of God, while marked by the peculiarities of culture, is a creaturely reality that reaches across cultures.

To praise God through song is to obey the first and greatest commandment: to love God "with all the heart, and with all the understanding, and with all the strength" (Mk. 12:33). Good singing requires the fusion of all our faculties. It takes the heart to focus our will and our emotion; it takes the understanding to shape a phrase and inflect the meaning; and it takes physical strength to support a column of air that will support the sound that supports the song that supports the praise of God. When we sing to God with all that we are, we are living what the psalmist commands: "Let everything that breathes praise the LORD! Praise the LORD!" (Ps. 150:6).

Sometimes we praise God through attentively listening to those more musically gifted than ourselves. But the doctrine of creation actualized through song makes it clear that any liturgical practice that does not allow adequately for the singing of the whole people of God is a truncated expression of biblical faith. Services that require the congregation only to listen and not to sing do not engage all of us for all of God. They effectively rewrite the end of Psalm 150. It no longer reads, "Let *everything* that breathes praise the Lord," but "Let *some* that breathe praise the Lord."

Principle Six: Singing Can Manifest Salvation

One of the saddest things that church musicians and pastors observe is those members of a congregation who never join in the singing. Their mouths shut, they stand silent while others sing around them. Sometimes there are physical reasons for silence, but other times it may be that the non-singers were told at an early age: "You cannot sing; just move your lips." The result is an inferiority complex about their voice so that they cannot bring themselves to join in the music. This is no small matter. It is a major blow that constricts an individual's means of communicating and connecting with others.

Reflecting on the experience of people haunted by childhood memories of being told they could not sing, W. A. Mathieu observes: "When we sing the heart is alive in the larynx, and that narrow channel is highly sensitive to aggression. It takes only a small blow to cause big damage. Some unconscious meanness, an offhand dig, might seem to a child like a slap on the heart, and the heart has a very long memory for pain."[43]

The memory of pain that diminishes our humanity needs the sensitive musical wisdom and training that W. A. Mathieu offers non-singers in *The Listening Book*. But it also requires a recognition of how the grace of God frees us to risk failure and mistakes. Without such liberation, salvation never becomes an effective reality in our lives.

> How shriveled, Lord, the soul
> that grips what it receives
> and dares not free its anxious hold
> but foolishly believes
> that you are too severe
> to pardon any loss,
> forgetting how your son made clear
> forgiveness on the cross.

Of course, we will make musical mistakes in the act of praising God. We human creatures are imperfect instruments for the praise of God. But if we cannot risk wrong notes in the adoration of God, we cannot risk wrong deeds in the service of God. If the guarantee of perfection were the prerequisite of discipleship, none of us would be able to do a single thing in the name of God.

A culture of entertainment feeds the suppression of congregational song. Accustomed to listening to singers whose performance is enhanced by electronic amplification and dazzling lighting effects, we come to think of our own voices as frail and inadequate. This is one of those places where the culture of the church needs to stand for a different set of values. God honors every voice lifted in the praise of God.

Congregational singing is a witness to our belief that worship is based not on the adequacy of our efforts, but on the saving, gracious character of the One we praise. A God who forgives sins certainly forgives wrong notes! As singing manifests our creaturehood, it also manifests our salvation. Our music is a sign that the saving grace of Christ is freeing us to do what we were created to do: to give ourselves with complete abandonment to God, not withholding our gifts because they are not as impressive as what we have heard and seen popular artists do.

Principle Seven: Church Song Is an Experience of Discipleship

Congregational music is a way of praying for the generosity of spirit that brings the abundant life of discipleship:

> From hearts that hide and hoard
> the treasures that you send
> free us, till we by faith, O Lord,
> shall act as you intend,
> till we risk all for you,
> risk everything you give,
> and risking, learn what Jesus knew:
> by risking all, we live.

Perhaps this act of risk is the more profound reason that adults love so much to hear the children sing in church. It is not only because the adults are proud parents or think the children cute, but because in that moment of watching and hearing the young ones open their mouths in the praise of God the adults remember their less cautious selves. Hearing the children, they reclaim the best hopes of their hearts: to risk all for Christ who is their way, their truth, their life. It is one of those times when the prophet's vision becomes true before our eyes and in our ears, "and a little child shall lead them" (Isa. 11:6), and we understand anew that "unless you change and become like children, you will never enter the kingdom of heaven" (Mt. 18:3).

Singing in church, then, not only manifests our creaturehood and salvation; it is also an experience of discipleship, a way of risking ourselves for Christ. To stand and sing in the community of faith is to begin to find the strength to stand for justice and compassion in the brutal world.

Principle Eight: The Full Expression of Faith Requires a Broad Spectrum of Music

We need a broad spectrum of music to express the fullness of the gospel, to remind ourselves of the global church and the whole human community. It is theologically inadequate to limit our musical selections to what is least challenging or most popular or what fits only within our culture's idea of music. The new hymnals of most denominations have greatly increased the repertoire of congregational song with additions from around the world, and the act of singing these songs, however imperfectly, is a way of reminding a congregation of God's care for all the peoples of the earth.

The greatest theologians have always refused to water down the gospel. Indeed, they have done the opposite: They have reminded us of the need for strenuous thinking, for a disciplined life of prayer, for a process of continually growing into the full maturity of Christ. If we insist on doing these things conceptually, but we constrict ecclesial sonic culture to what is easy and familiar, we will, in effect, be saying, "*Talk* all you want about the demands of discipleship, but do not embody them in the song and sound of worship."

It would be ironic and tragic if the church simplified the embodiment of the gospel in worship while other religious movements and quasi-religious disciplines such as athletics continued to become more and more demanding on people's God-given talents. As Paul Westermeyer, drawing on the work of Martin Marty, observes, "The church at many points appears to have lost its nerve and the sense that its message is worth a comparable effort [comparable to the other demanding disciplines people undertake] or that people deserve what is worth the effort, assuming that only what sells immediately has any value."[44] Westermeyer's words alert us to the need for a broad ecclesial sonic culture in order to be more expressive of the fullness of God. Such a culture is open to popular, easily accessible musical idioms, but it also insists on the need for more demanding and enduring music that calls us to use all of us for all of God. A broad-based sonic culture honors Paul's principle that the body of Christ needs to make room for the astonishing variety of gifts that the Spirit supplies (1 Corinthians 12).

Integrating Cultural Humility and Pride

There are many other doctrines and principles I might have invoked in formulating a theological understanding of the church's sonic culture. But my purpose has been to model a way of going about the task rather than to promote one definitive philosophy. As you develop your own theological understanding of the role of music in the life of worship, it would be helpful to keep in mind Sigvald Tveit's wisdom about two different extremes in making judgments about congregational song. Tveit warns that we may regard our own culture as "uninteresting and inferior," *or* we may consider it to be "superior" while "other traditions have little to contribute in comparison."[45] Tveit reflects:

> Both of these extremes are negative: self-depreciation in the first case is as invidious as the egocentricity of the other is unpleasant. Humility can co-exist with pride in our traditions, while love for our heritage ought to be linked to curiosity and respect for other people's culture...The Golden Mean suggests that we be both attentive to the experiences of others and the treasures of their cultures, while remaining conscious of our own.[46]

Tveit's grace of soul suggests the more profound depths of the debates about church music. Sometimes we may be ready to throw up our hands in disgust and wish we did not have to deal with these matters. But by placing the debates in the context of the interrelationship of culture, preaching, and worship, we see that we are dealing with matters at the heart of the gospel: achieving mutual understanding and reconciliation. It is not fair to ask church musicians to bear alone the burden of this demanding work. Expanding, sustaining, and interpreting an ecclesial sonic culture requires that worship committees, pastors, and musicians work together as colleagues. It also requires affirmation of the musicians for what they are doing in a time of cultural fragmentation. Therefore, I conclude this chapter with a prayer of gratitude for those who lead us into the songful praise of God even while we wrestle with multiple sonic cultures.

> Source of all that is good and true and beautiful,
> to whom whales and birds and crickets sing,
> keep constant in your musicians
> the conviction that your Spirit works through them
> to reach a vast and varied host of souls
> who gather in church
> for hope, assurance, grace, beauty,
> for some sign of your care,
> for solace from grief and loss,
> for strength to stand for justice,
> for a glimpse of wonder and mystery,
> for response to a need so hidden that it is known to
>   you alone.

Assure your musicians
that the rehearsals they lead,
the anthems they conduct,
the hymns they play,
the psalms they accompany,
the service music they offer,
the solos they sing,
the instrumental works they perform,
the programs they organize,
the words of encouragement they give
are again and again
the vessel of your Spirit
for healing the bruised, the lost, the broken
and for setting free
the holy aspirations of the human heart.

And since the souls that are saved
by the secret ministries of music
often find it too self-revealing,
too frightening,
to offer their thanks in person,
may their unarticulated gratitude
be gathered by the wind of your Spirit
and be borne to the hearts of your musicians
as a gift to renew their faith
so that they may continue to be instruments
of proclamation and pastoral care
as they lead your people
in singing your everlasting praise
through Jesus Christ our Lord, Amen.

4

BODY

If this were a chapter in a medical textbook about human anatomy, I might describe what our bodies have in common: the bones of the skeleton, tendons and muscles, the placement of organs, and the mechanics of physical movement. The focus would be on the animal materiality of us human beings. But a purely anatomical description, no matter how scientifically accurate, would not begin to account for the astounding variety of ways that human beings use their bodies to express their identities, to signal their social cohesion, and to communicate with one another. Gesture, posture, facial expression, and the amount of distance maintained between bodies vary enormously with culture.

Culture as the Mastery of a Somatic Idiom

Although the use of our bodies falls within certain biophysical limitations—for example, the direction in which we can bend our joints—we acquire a repertoire of bodily motions from the culture in which we live. A large part of growing up involves mastering what our elders consider to be the appropriate and inappropriate use of our bodies. They teach us the somatic idiom of our culture. By somatic idiom I mean the specific repertoire of posture, gesture, and facial expression that culture implants in our very being. Because we assume our particular somatic idiom to be natural, to be a part of the way things are, it is challenging to change how we use our bodies in a social setting.

> From its earliest moments a child is taught how to control and use its limbs, what it is to smile or frown, how to sit and stand, walk and talk; what constitutes respectful or disrespect-ful behavior toward elders and superiors; what it is to exer-cise choice or to make jokes; what tasks are appropriate to which genders, ages, social and economic classes. All of these practices shape the body in the most literal sense: disposi-tions to smile or frown carve lines upon the face, muscles in tongues and limbs develop knacks of speaking and walking, different tasks produce calluses in different places, mould spines in different ways. Through such practices which shape its body, a child develops and expresses its own individual-ity, and comes at the same time to incorporate the identity of its family, class, community: what it is to be a person, a child, a girl, a woman, a boy, a man; what it is to aspire to or occupy the status of labourer or manager.[1]

Because we start learning these things before we speak and long before we can reason as an adult, they lie deep in the bone, in the very nature of who we are.

> All bodily practices, such as talking, walking, reading and writing, are appropriated by repetition over time. Bodies are shaped, "memory" incorporated, by familiarization through time with movements in space, of eye or hand, lip or limb; in time and over time, instruction, explanation, commen-tary becomes unnecessary. With the habitual skill are incor-porated human values and dispositions which, in time and over time, come to be "natural." Such knowledge is largely unspoken: literally embodied, profoundly, secretly effective...so the power of bodily practices to constitute "memories" of past experiences depends, paradoxically, on their remaining unreflected upon and, apparently, "natural."[2]

The sense of our bodily practices being "natural" is an important element in how we communicate with one another in our native culture. The "naturalness" facilitates communication and relationship between all the members of a society who share the same repertoire of gestures and looks. Thomas Hardy offers a vivid example of this principle through his description of rural British culture at the end of the nineteenth century:

The yeomen, farmers, dairymen, and townsfolk, who came
to transact business in these ancient streets, spoke in other
ways than by articulation. Not to hear the words of your
interlocutor in metropolitan centers is to know nothing of
his meaning. Here the face, the arms, the hat, the stick, the
body throughout spoke equally with the tongue. To express
satisfaction the Casterbridge market-man added to his utter-
ance a broadening of the cheeks, a crevicing of the eyes, a
throwing back of the shoulders, which was intelligible from
the other end of the street.[3]

Notice the contrast between cultures: The person raised in a
"metropolitan" culture depends so entirely on words that meaning
cannot be communicated without language. But the rural folk whom
Hardy describes "transact business" through the way they use their
faces and bodies. Their somatic idiom is equal "with the tongue."
Just imagine the frustrations that would result for both parties if a
visitor from Hardy's "metropolitan centers" attempted to transact
business with one of his rural citizens!

The Challenge of Changing Our Somatic Idiom

If we try to change our patterns of posture, gesture, and facial
expression, our minds may say yes while our bodies say no. For our
bodies have a deeper, longer, and more persistent memory than our
adult reason. Thus, when I was eating noodles in Japan and my friends
asked me to slurp my noodles as was their custom (chap. 1), I mustered
only the faintest sucking sound and quickly returned to eating my
food silently. I was eager to join in their way of ingesting noodles, but
the memory of my body as formed by my Anglo American culture
overruled my desire to please my hosts.

Consider another example: the introduction of liturgical dance
into a tradition that for centuries has used a minimal amount of bodily
action in its worship. Let us say that its repertoire of liturgical bodily
actions is limited to the choir and ministers processing in, the
congregation standing for hymns, sitting for the rest of the service,
bowing their heads for prayer, and passing the collection plates and
communion elements. It would be wrong to conclude that such
worship does not engage the body. Sitting for a long period is a highly
physical activity—just ask someone whose back gives out during a
long sermon! But it is a particular use of the body, very different
from watching someone bend, sway, and twirl down the aisle and
very different from inviting the congregation to participate by imitating
the gestures of a leader standing up front.

Even if we are members of a worship committee that has decided our service needs to feature more physical movement, even if the liturgical dancer or leader of congregational movement is excellent, even if we rationally understand all the theological and pastoral reasons for a more dynamic use of the body in the praise of God, even with all these things in place, when we participate in the service we may feel awkward. Our bodies may send a message to our mind that we are violating some sacred norm, acting in a forbidden way. We might not tell anybody, and we might try to reason ourselves out of our reaction, but the resistance, the judgment that the dance is wrong, would persist.

Our resistance may not arise because we are bad or unimaginative or uptight or closed to trying new things. Frequently, it originates in our childhood training about the right and wrong ways to use the body. The dance does not feel "natural" to us. Of course, one of the wonderful things about human beings is that God made us to be adaptive, and if we keep coming to worship and continue to watch the dancer and try the motions, then over time we may settle into the liturgical movements and even come to love them. Just as it is possible to learn a foreign language, it is possible to learn a new somatic idiom. But we need to be gentle with ourselves and with others by allowing for the expression of resistance. Making people feel bad for the way their culture has shaped them is not an effective way of opening them up to new forms of somatic expression.

The Inescapable Importance of Our Somatic Idiom

Whatever our upbringing, we cannot afford to ignore the importance of the use of the body in worship. As Jyoti Sahi has observed, there are profound theological and political consequences to living in a culture that acts as if we humans can transcend the materiality of our creaturehood.

> Our body sensations and feeling must not be ignored. Spirituality can easily degenerate into a kind of elitist gnosticism that denies the importance of the physical—which means ultimately a denial of the incarnation. By looking for renewed insights in the cultural traditions of those who have been often marginalized and oppressed, we are once again giving importance to that which is close to the earth, the elemental forces which are very real to those who depend on the basic necessities of life. Those who have no need to struggle for existence live in a kind of luxury which increasingly estranges

them from the elemental. Fire, water, wind, earth are no longer perceived as essential. Those who become wealthy and refined forget that their very wealth derives from the oppression of the poor.[4]

No matter how splendid our sermons on the goodness of creation (Genesis 1) and on the incarnation (John 1), a disembodied liturgy may imply through its paucity of somatic expression the opposite message: The world is not good, and the Word did not become flesh. By effectively reversing the central affirmations of biblical faith about creation and incarnation and thereby estranging us from what Sahi terms "the elemental," our worship, instead of helping us to discern the deeper meaning and purpose of our existence, may contribute to individual and social anomie. Nathan Mitchell, drawing on the work of Erik Erikson, concludes:

> We become human…by learning the ritual repertoire of the human community. Thus, a decay or perversion of effective rituals creates a public and private void—a crisis of meaning and value—that may lead to violence or rage. When a culture loses "the gift of imparting values by meaningful ritualization," Erikson warned, the result is neurosis, social disorder, chaos and conflict.[5]

For Christians, learning "the ritual repertoire" of the church is a way of establishing, deepening, and expanding our relationship to God. I enter church, kneel, and make the sign of the cross. The repeated actions over the years begin to shape my character. Entering church becomes a way of entering the awareness of how miniscule my knowledge is. Kneeling reinforces my astonishment that there is anything at all instead of just nothingness. Making the sign of cross, I sense anew a point of convergence within me and all that lives with the workings of holy love. These may not be your ritual actions—you may come from an ecclesial culture with a different somatic idiom—but whatever "the ritual repertoire" of your church, it is shaping your relationship to God.

It may be that the current pressures to revitalize worship arise from an awareness that the somatic paucity of our ritual life in church contributes to the atrophy of a vital faith. Finding fresh words for preaching, prayer, and song cannot alone address the need of human beings to construct a world of meaning. It also requires an adequate repertoire of posture, gesture, and movement. These needs are built into us as bodily creatures raised in a particular culture.

A body "re-members" its identity. That is to say, it discovers and reinvents, enforces and reinforces its identity, and in this way gives "life" to its members—or takes "life" away; life, that is, "as it is lived" by members of the myriad interlocking, overlapping, multi-layered, and conflicting groupings that constitute a human community. Postures and gestures characteristic of a class, of a whole people, are inherited; family traits are passed on—familiar and yet individual.[6]

If our sacred rituals do not allow for adequate somatic engagement, it decreases the effectiveness of our ritual "re-membering"—of reassembling all the memories that are stored in our bodies as well as our minds and hearts. We are left hungering for a more fully embodied expression of our deepest yearnings for God.

Conflicts over Somatic Idiom

Once we decide to use our bodies more actively in worship, we are faced with the conflicting values of different cultures. Consider, for example, passing the peace. If everyone in the congregation shares the same somatic idiom, the liturgical action proceeds smoothly and easily. But look what happens when there is wide range of different traditions about the use of the body. A simple action becomes a complex dilemma. Some people have been raised in cultures that consider hugging to be an appropriate public gesture even among strangers. Others have been raised to shake hands but not to hug in public. Put a hugger next to a hand shaker in the same pew, and any sense of the peace of the Lord may evaporate. The spiritual energies of both may be consumed with trying to figure out how to negotiate their differences. It is difficult to do. The hugger may interpret the hand shaker's distance as coldness or aloofness. The hand shaker may interpret the hugger's approach as a violation of personal space. How can the peace of the Lord be embodied when the inculcated patterns of embodiment are at odds with each other?

Or consider the large number of preachers who in recent years have moved out of pulpits to stand on the chancel steps or to walk among the congregation as they deliver their sermons. Some congregations have joyfully accepted and even encouraged this change. But other congregations and preachers insist that sermons must be delivered from the pulpit. There are listeners who want the preacher close, and listeners who want the preacher farther away.

The Use of the Body in the Bible

How to use bodies and where to position bodies have been major questions throughout the history of worship. Othmar Keel has collected images of ancient worshipers that are drawn from archeological sites around the Mediterranean basin.[7] The volume reveals an immense variety of posture, gesture, and facial expression that the author relates to the psalms. To somebody like me, who has prayed and sung the psalms all his life, there is a moment of startling insight when I read the familiar words placed as captions under these dramatic physical poses. Language gives way to the reality it invokes: human creatures using face, limbs, and torso to communicate with God.

Four weeping women on their knees—two bowed low, and two sitting back on their legs with their hands raised to their heads—are a gripping testimonial to ritualized grief.[8] Two of the women have broad streams of water flowing from their eyes. The power of this depiction is so great that it becomes difficult to distance myself from their grief, a distance more easily achieved if all I had were the words: "I went about as one who laments for a mother, bowed down and in mourning" (Ps. 35:14). Lament is more than a word. Lament is an action of the body. Lament is kneeling and bowing and raising hands and pouring forth a stream of tears from the eyes. The picture arises from a culture that has ritualized the full use of the body in the expression of grief.

In another picture seven women dance, leap, and skip in the praise of God. One lifts her hands toward heaven, another to her forehead, while the rest are swinging and swaying their arms. The uniformity of their leaps, the bearing of their bodies, and the similarities in their attire and headdress suggest that this is highly proscribed ritual behavior. "You have turned my mourning into dancing; you have taken off my sackcloth and clothed me with joy" (Ps. 30:11). Dancing and gladness are no longer merely words on a page. They are human creatures in motion. They are energy, rhythm, and pulsation. The picture arises from a culture that has ritualized the full use of the body in the expression of joy.

A man in profile bows face down to the earth. Beneath the ground, indicated by a thick, bold black line, are dozens of wavy lines representing water. Growing up through the water and the solar plexus of the prostrate figure is a verdant tree, lush with hanging fruit.[9] "They are like trees planted by streams of water" (Ps. 1:3a). The familiar metaphor begins to flow with the juice and sap of a real tree, and prayer is transformed from speech into a posture of obeisance. The figure acknowledges the Divine with his entire physical being. The picture arises from a culture that has ritualized the full use of the body in the expression of prayer.

I have covered only three pictures out of the nearly five hundred in Keel's book, but three are enough to give an idea of the rich use of the body that marked the cultures that shaped the writers of the Hebrew Scriptures and out of which their words about worship, prayer, lament, and praise arose. I contrast their extensive repertoire of gesture, posture, movement, and facial expression with something I read in the bulletin of a church I once attended as a visitor: "Worship is thinking right thoughts about God." I had just read that statement when the service began with the call to worship spoken from the back of the sanctuary: "O come, let us worship and bow down, let us kneel before the LORD, our Maker!" (Ps. 95:6). Nobody knelt, nobody bowed. All we did was sit and listen to the words, hopefully "thinking right thoughts about God." Sitting, as I have already pointed out, is doing something with our bodies, but it is clearly not what the psalmist commands us to do. The ancient words remain the same, but the somatic idiom has changed.

Then the hymn was announced, and we stood to sing. Standing is the exact opposite of what the psalmist asks us to do! The contrast would have been even greater if the worship leader had used the more literal translation of the *New English Bible*: "Come! Let us throw ourselves at his feet in homage, let us kneel before the LORD who made us; for he is our God." A highly rational ecclesial culture had transfigured the psalmist's call to worship from a material, bodily action into an invisible process of thought. There is nothing wrong with thought! But if you doubt how differently thought proceeds according to the somatic idiom that accompanies it, act out with your body what the psalmist commands. Instead of sitting motionless while you recite the words of the psalmist, throw yourself at the feet of God; kneel down. It changes what goes on in your brain because when you use your body in different ways, different electrical circuits are engaged in your cranium.

When Body Is the Measure of Belief

Our theological debates are often about the meaning of words and what constitutes right belief. But members of the ancient cultures that gave birth to our beliefs would be baffled by our preoccupation with words. Of course they honored words, or they would not have preserved their texts so carefully. But it is important to remember that the vast majority of people did not read, and writing was the privilege of relatively few. We distort ancient cultures when we fail to allow adequately for the other "languages" by which people expressed their relationship to God, including their somatic idioms. Hearing our wordiness, they might well wonder,

- What about our bodies?
- How are we using them in the worship of God?

These were in fact the much more important questions for early Christians, especially in relationship to the surrounding cultures that expected everybody to participate in rituals that venerated the emperor or the state deities.

> The new religionists [early Christians] refused to worship the gods and Caesar, hence outsiders concluded correctly that they were *asebeis* and *atheoi*. It was their behavior, not their beliefs, that earned Christians these epithets...Outsiders must have found the public behavior (nonconformity) of the new religionists queer and unsettling. By their nonparticipation in public cults, Christians offended ancient and highly revered customs deeply rooted in Greco-Roman society. Whatever beliefs they held in private was their business—government or socially imposed thought control in this realm was nonexistent. But, like everyone else, Christians were expected to conform in public, and their refusal to do so naturally enkindled speculations and ignited suspicions of various sorts, atheism included.[10]

The suspicion and persecution of the early church arose from the refusal of Christians to use their bodies in the way that the surrounding culture expected of everyone. Christians were free to think whatever they wanted to think. It was the failure to use their bodies in the physical acts of paying homage to rulers and deities of the state that brought them into disrepute.

There is some ancient writing that claims Christians *did* conform to the prevailing behaviors of the surrounding culture. An anonymous Christian wrote to the imperial procurator of Egypt around 200 C.E. explaining:

> Christians distinguish themselves from other people not by nationality or by language or by dress. They do not inhabit their own cities or use a special language or practice a life that makes them distinctive or conspicuous...They live in Greek and barbarian cities, following the lot that each has

chosen, and they conform to indigenous customs in matters
of clothing and food and the rest of life.[11]

The letter may be an apologetic attempt to portray the new religion
in terms acceptable to the authorities. Eager to win tolerance for
Christians, the author makes them out to be more conforming than
they are. But whether the letter is a prevarication to win acceptance
or a description of actual practices, it gives witness to the ancient
cultural significance of the body.

The letter also mentions "clothing and food." How we dress and
what we eat are part of our somatic idiom. What did Christians wear?
What did they eat? These were issues for the church long before
200 c.e. The pastorals address the need for women to cover their
heads, and Paul adjudicates a dispute about food offered to idols.
These scriptural concerns mark the beginning of a complex process
of transforming the use of the body in the early church. As the gospel
spread around the Mediterranean basin,

> the elite culture of classical Greek and Roman philosophies
> was adapted by the Christian philosopher-theologians, who
> were the leaders of the Christian church, to people like Cicero
> and Augustine. Body motions were regulated by modera-
> tion *(modestia)*. Excesses (or gesticulations) were outlawed.
> In this universe of belief and reflection, the body was held
> suspect. It was fallen and an instrument of sin. Any display
> considered immodest or excessive was removed from the
> liturgy. This explains the exclusion of dance from the Ro-
> man liturgy. God-like immobility or the absence of emotion
> was preferred to the "un-discipline" flexing of the body. Im-
> mobility symbolized perfection. God is the unmoved
> mover.[12]

Note here the profound theological implications of a culture's
somatic idiom. Nothing less than the nature of God and human
identity are expressed through the way the body is used. Therefore,
early church writers can be vitriolic in their attacks on what they
consider to be ungodly movement of the body, such as Arnobius (d.
circa 330 c.e.), who fumes with anger:

> Was it for this that he sent souls, that as members of a holy
> and dignified race they practice here the arts of music and
> piping...under the influence of which a multitude of other
> lascivious souls abandon themselves to bizarre movements
> of the body, dancing and singing, forming rings of dancers,

and ultimately raising their buttocks and hips to sway with the rippling motion of their loins?[13]

Sometimes there were appeals to a supposedly golden past when reserve and decorum reigned in the use of the body. Thus, the famous preacher John Chrysostom (circa 347–407 C.E.) calls into question the dramatic music and dance that had evidently begun to be a part of some Christian weddings:

> Do you not see with what dignity weddings were celebrated in antiquity? Hear this, you who flutter after Satan's pomp and who from the very start dishonor the nuptial solemnities. Were there auloi [double reeded instruments employed in the orgiastic rites of Dionysus] there? Were there cymbals, or diabolical dances? For what reason, tell me, do you straightway bring such shame into your house, and summon people from the stage and orchestra pit, so that with extravagant expense you spoil the modesty of the maiden and make the groom more wanton.[14]

The extravagant use of the body illustrated by Othmar Keel's book contrasts with the philosophical ideal of "moderation." Hence, we cannot make an appeal to the Bible and tradition to establish a single authoritative standard for what constitutes the right use of the body in our worship and preaching. Ancient witness, spanning many centuries and cultures, reveals a vast range of somatic idiom, from ecstatic dance to restraint.

Major Tensions about the Body in the History of Christian Worship

Despite its rich variety, the history of the use of the body in Christian worship is also marked by an extreme limitation: namely, the failure to incorporate fully women as living, bodily creatures.

> Two constants governed the place of women in Christian worship throughout history; first their exclusion from the priesthood, which was conditioned by their gender and secondly the tabu of menstruation (which was less so). Both these led to specific ways in which women were excluded from certain spheres of liturgical life.[15]

Once again we see that the bodily practices of the church have theological ramifications. Excluding one-half of the human race from full bodily participation in every aspect of the church's worship life results in a constricted and distorted theological anthropology. It also feeds a species of religious language and imagery that are at odds with the grandest visions of what God has done through Christ so that

> concerns specific to women are underrepresented in the liturgy: for example, we recognize freedom from circumcision as an important symbol of the universality of salvation, but women were never circumcised as a sign of their reception into the Jewish faith community. Thus freedom from circumcision as an image for the universality of salvation is an image which fundamentally excludes women: this is not helpful if we are concerned to clarify the universality of salvation.[16]

The Bible and tradition reveal, then, at least two major tensions about the use of the body in worship. One is the wide repertoire of somatic idiom, varying from dramatic posture and gesture to an insistence on moderation and reserve. The other tension results from including women in the community but not admitting them to full participation because female bodies are different from male bodies. Both tensions surface again and again in the history of Christian worship and continue into the present day.

Ambivalence about the Place of the Female Body in Christian Worship

Because the body's memory goes back to our early childhood, long before the development of our capacity for rational thought, the body may sometimes contradict what we believe with our heads. I recall, for example, the first female preaching students I had in my homiletics classes, more than twenty-five years ago. Some of them, even though they were convinced of their calling and were gifted as preachers, would tell me they had difficulty picturing themselves in the pulpit or even delivering their sermons from the chancel steps. There was no question about their commitment to ordination and full participation of women in church leadership. They felt passionately about it, and they provided sound theological reasoning to support their position. Yet when it came to stepping into the role of preacher, there was something that made them hesitate. Together we discovered that reasoning about it did not dissolve the resistance. Only by creating a classroom that felt like a "safe place" and having them step into the role of preacher was the resistance overcome.

I believe that what they were encountering in themselves was the residue of their upbringing in an ecclesial culture of male leadership. The women had long overcome that culture's gender limitations in their minds, but they found its biases were still present in the memory of their bodies. As children they had not seen and heard women preach. They had seen and heard only male preachers, and the congregations to whom those men preached often consisted of more women than men. From the time they were girls, those women seminarians had observed the male body standing and delivering sermons, while female bodies sat and received what the males had to say. Thus, when the women stepped up to preach their first sermon, even though they were intellectually convinced of the words they were about to speak, the body whispered hesitation into the heart. Over time, however, as they preached again and again and saw and heard other women preach, their bodies relinquished the culturally implanted resistance, and they could bring their fully integrated selves into the act of preaching.

In more recent years, I have had a number of female preaching students in their early to mid-twenties. Some of these women grew up with women pastors. They are the beneficiaries of the women who were in seminary twenty-five years ago. Male leadership did not dominate the ecclesial culture of this new generation, and as a result they do not have the same hesitancy about stepping into the pulpit or onto the chancel steps to deliver their sermons. Their bodies are more ready to move into the role because that role has been open to both females and males during the formative years of childhood when the deepest somatic memories are being shaped.

The inner hesitation of those first women preaching students illumines the tenacity of resistance to female leadership that is often manifest in the church. The transformation of those women students demonstrates that intellectual arguments alone—as essential as they are—will not transform an ecclesial culture dominated by male leadership. It is only when the intellectual understanding is fused with a new somatic repertoire that the culture is transformed. Not just thinking ideas, but standing to preach forever changed those women by changing the somatic idiom of their lives and the lives of the communities that saw and heard them.

In the case of the women preachers, the mind and heart took the lead, and the body later followed. However, the process of transformation can also work in reverse. During the same time period that I was observing the struggles of women seminarians, I was frequently visiting churches throughout the United States and Canada to lead conferences and to preach. I recall many laywomen and laymen who recounted that they had initially been opposed to the ordination of women, but then a female pastor came to lead their church. Hearing and seeing her preach and receiving the sacrament from her hands, they discovered that their intellectual and emotional arguments against women clergy vanished. In these cases the body took the lead, and the mind and heart followed.

The transformation of the women preaching students and the conversion of the laity reveal that it is possible to rewrite the script that the body has memorized. It is often hard work, even frightening in its initial stages, but it is possible. Transformation is possible because God has created us to be adaptable, and it is also possible because within the patriarchal culture of the church, there has always been an undercurrent of the feminine that keeps surfacing even when it is denied by authoritative doctrine and teaching. Early Christian artwork gives tangible expression to these feminine forces.

> Whether women commonly experienced Christ as a woman is difficult to ascertain, since written sources so seldom preserve the reflections of women in the Early Christian period. But perhaps what is lacking in literary sources has been made up in the visual sources. it is not unlikely that many of the sacrophagi were commissioned by women—wives or widows—and that the imagery reflects their visions. Perhaps this is why the feminine Christ is so frequent in that medium. In the Traditio Legis sarcophagus in Arles the union of male and female has been expressed in a figure of Christ who is both an old man and a woman.[17]

The visual representation of the faith in the early centuries of Christianity manifests a valuing of the feminine body that was in many cases in conflict with what the church fathers wrote. Margaret Miles demonstrates that the contradictions lying between written and visual sources may represent different constellations of power within the culture of the early church. Miles acknowledges that those who have mastered reading and writing and who become the leading "language users" of a culture do, in fact, possess considerable power, "Yet it cannot be assumed that their power and influence are total, or even representative, within their culture."[18] Thus, it is inadequate to appeal only to written resources in understanding the place of woman's body in the life of the early church. "We must anticipate that the use of a different kind of historical evidence, visual images, may reveal the presence of even more fundamental contradictions and conflicts than are identifiable with the exclusive use of verbal texts."[19]

Miles's historical observation reframes the transformation of male-dominated ecclesial culture that I traced through the stories of the women seminarians and the laity who were converted to the ordination and leadership of women as pastors. The women and the laity were working with an ambivalence about the female body that has been present from the earliest centuries of the faith. The women and laity had inherited through language, custom, and somatic idiom the ambiguities of their forebears. Their struggles at cultural transformation flowed from two thousand years of ambivalence about the place of the female body in the church.

Early church leaders were aware of the threat posed by the popularity of images that offered a "dangerously wide spectrum of interpretations of God's activity of creation, incarnation, and redemption."[20] But the church's chief language users were unable to suppress the feminine that kept asserting itself through visual images.

> Alongside his virile manifestations, Christ in Early Christian art often showed a decidedly feminine aspect which we over-look at our own risk...once this feminine aspect of Christ had gained an acceptability, later artists, whether in the Middle Ages or beyond, felt free to exploit it without apologies. Judging from the rich tradition of effeminate imagery of Christ, it appears that people were not uncomfortable with such a Savior.[21]

Not uncomfortable with a feminine Christ, some of our forbears also presented the Trinity in a way that honored the female as well as the male body. For example, in the Urschalling Church, southwest of Munich, there is a painting of the Trinity from around 1300. A haloed and bearded father God on the right and a haloed and bearded Jesus on the left flank the Holy Spirit, a haloed and very feminine woman in a soft, flowing dress.

What emerges from history is a continuous story of ambivalence about the place of the female body in the expression of faith and the ministry of the church. When we encounter this ambivalence in ourselves and in others, we are facing something greater than the biases and customs of our own era, something greater than the conflicts of our individual psyches, something greater than the stubbornness of our denominational and congregational structures. We are dealing with conflicts inherited from the ecclesial cultures of the past.

If we are going to appeal to the past as a source of illumination, then we must open ourselves to the multiple expressions of faith that characterize our history. By doing this, we will find that our forebears are more helpful to our self-understanding than we initially dreamed. For the place of the female body in the ministry of the church is not monochromatic and consistent, especially when we compare the somatic idiom of the church's imagery to its written doctrine. Then we are able to trace in our ancestors' corporate life the very tensions that exist inside ourselves and among our communities. Having identified how deep down and far back the roots reach, we may more fully understand why it feels like radical surgery when we begin to change the somatic idiom of our culture.

Tensions between Somatic Idioms of Moderation and Extravagance

Just as the church's language users were not able to eliminate the manifestation of the feminine body in the expression of faith, so also they failed in their efforts to limit the motion of the body to modest gestures and postures.

> The motions of the hand and face, very prominent in rhetorics, were the commonly approved gestures. Of course this elite Christian culture was difficult to apply on the popular level. But any admission of popular practices into the liturgy was under the watchful eye of the minority clerical elite. These gestures were not indifferent. They embody the Greco-Roman Christian world.[22]

It appears that there were two different somatic idioms representing two different cultures in the church. One was the somatic idiom of restraint and modesty. Such bodily expression was congruent with the church's rhetoric and with the values of reason and moderation that were championed by Greek and Roman schools of philosophy and public decorum. This approach, however, was not easily enforced on the general populace, who gave themselves to what the elite considered to be an excessive use of the body.

The tension between elite and popular cultures is manifest in fourth-century criticism of Christian art, which was characterized by a desire "to make the accessibility of their faith visually apparent," resulting in the charge that Christians suffered "a lack of standards and requirements, moral and intellectual."[23] This is a tension that returns again and again in history as people from various cultures employ a different species of motions and gestures to express their faith. The charge of "a lack of standards and requirements, moral and intellectual" is a recurrent judgment made by one culture against another when they observe their differing somatic idioms. Just as we saw shifts in the history of music in Christian worship, so too there have been continual transformations of its somatic idiom, and that has left plenty of opportunity for judgments to be made! It would be possible to write an entire book on the shifting somatic idioms of Christian worship and the accompanying judgments of one group against the other. But rather than attempt such a full history here, I hold up a few representative examples that will help us to put the way we use our bodies in a much broader context.

> In antique art, Roman and late Hellenistic, there is a great tradition of raising a symbolic object, showing it to everybody who is there to see, as an act of triumphal proclamation. Let me stress that this is not a mere gesture, a spontaneous movement of the body, such as raising the hand, but the symbolic act of lifting up an object endowed with a socially accepted meaning.[24]

Such use of the body is technically called "ceremonial"; that is to say, it is a formalized gesture that the congregation considers to be a significant expression of its faith and practice. Ceremonial acts serve "to communicate what we might call an institutional intention, which is understood by a whole community, unlike an idiosyncratic intention which is susceptible to being understood by the one [who] makes it and the one at the receiving end."[25]

Ceremonial acts, because they are not spontaneous but ritually orchestrated, tend to be more restrained and modest. If they were done suddenly or out of context, they would not possess the power granted to them by the community. Indeed, the misplacing of the gesture from the ritual to which it belongs would strike the devout as sacrilegious.

Consider, for example, the elevation of the chalice or host during the celebration of the mass, a ceremonial gesture that by the twelfth or thirteenth century had come to invoke "adoration and worship."[26] For millions of living Christian worshipers this ceremonial gesture continues to have the same impact centuries after its meaning was firmly established. But if a priest who elevated the host during the eucharist were later to repeat the same gesture while passing bread at a dinner party, people would be puzzled if not offended. The ritual context that authorizes the ceremonial gesture and gives it power and meaning would be missing, and so the gesture might be taken as a spoof or parody on what is holy.

On the other hand, someone raised in a culture whose somatic idiom is self-consciously anti-ceremonial might be offended by the elevation of the bread in a service of worship. I recall here a Protestant minister who along with dozens of other ministers and priests had been invited to attend a Roman Catholic mass and to join completely in participating. He was very upset afterwards that the ecumenical group had attended, because the priest had elevated the host. The clergyman's reaction was not purely personal. He explained that some of his ancestors had five centuries earlier lost their lives for standing against this "idolatrous action." Five centuries may seem like a long time to hold onto such a memory. After all, have we not all moved on intellectually and socially? The very fact that a Roman Catholic priest would invite an ecumenical group of ministers and priests to participate fully in the mass is surely a sign of the great advances we have made since the religious wars when the ancestors of many of these groups were killing one another in the name of God. At the level of thought and dialogue, five hundred years seems a long stretch of time. Knowing how graciously the clergyman had discussed a wide range of ideas in the past, I would not have expected the strong reaction.

But we were no longer dealing in ideas alone. We were participating in ceremonial action, in a somatic idiom different from his own, and these realities go deeper than ideas. Five centuries is not long when the memory has been kept alive not only in the heart but in the body. I could hear the hurt in the man's voice, a blend of fear and anger that was inculcated in him by an ecclesial culture whose somatic idiom was steadfastly against the use of the ceremonial. The body preserves the memory with a vividness and tenacity that ideas alone will never achieve.

The story demonstrates why reaching across cultures involves so much more than thinking and talking. It helps us understand the depth of conflict and judgment over the church's somatic idiom that has erupted again and again in its history. These difficulties arose not only over the use of the body in celebrating sacraments but also over the use of the body in preaching. What is the appropriate posture for a preacher? for the congregation that is receiving the sermon? How much movement should a preacher use in the delivery of a sermon, and how much should the congregation use in responding? These all involve the somatic idiom of particular ecclesial cultures.

The appropriate posture for a preacher has changed over the centuries. "In modern Christian churches the congregation sits and the minister stands to preach, but in the early Church it was exactly the opposite: the people stood and the preacher sat. His seat or *cathedra* was the symbol of his authority, every bit as much as the *stella curulis* was the symbol of imperial authority."[27] This somatic idiom goes far back beyond the time of Christ. Othmar Keel explains:

"To stand" means "to be ready" to respond instantly to every inclination of the king (or the god) and to fulfill his wishes. In Israel's later history, God's will as expressed in the Torah became more and more *the* determinative of Israel's experience of God. Therefore, "standing" as it related to this experience became the expression for divine service in general.[28]

Keel accompanies his verbal descriptions with scenes that feature highly stylized gestures between supplicants and kings or deities. The king or deity usually sits straight up on the throne. There is no slouching or informality. One arm, bent at the elbow, is extended outward and slanted slightly upwards with the hand open and revealing the palm, a gesture that may express greeting or blessing. There is sometimes in these pictures an intermediary figure, a priest or lesser deity, who is leading a worshiper by the hand to the throne of the god. Both the intermediary and the worshiper lift up one of their hands in a gesture that to us looks like someone swearing to tell the truth in a court of law. The symmetry and balance of these pictures suggest a highly formalized ceremonial action set within a clear hierarchal structure:

- a god who has power
- an intermediary who facilitates an approach to the powerful one
- the worshiper who comes as a supplicant and servant.

Examining these pictures, there is no question about how the body is to be used. It is impossible to imagine the suppliant releasing the hand of the intermediary and spontaneously running forward to hug the deity. Such behavior would be tantamount to attacking the universe of meaning that the gestures, movement, and arrangement of the bodies express. The somatic idiom is nothing less than the manifestation of the divine order as understood by the communities that produced these striking iconographic records of their liturgical practices.

Although to our eyes these ancient images may seem to come from another planet, they in fact capture something about the ceremonial use of the body that many traditions still incorporate into their worship. Consider, for example, Christian traditions whose confirmation and ordination ceremonies include a candidate, a sponsor, and a bishop or other denominational official. A frequent pattern is that the bishop sits in a chair atop the chancel steps, a sponsor steps forward in order to present the candidate, and the candidate then approaches the bishop. If we were to make a line drawing of the ceremony and place it next to one of Keel's ancient images, the formal arrangement of the bodies and in some cases even the gestures would be strikingly similar.

The persistence of the ceremonial across so many centuries suggests that it arises from deep springs in human nature. However, there is another somatic idiom that can run just as deeply through a culture: a highly dramatic use of the body in preaching and worship that contrasts sharply with the reserve and moderation characteristic of the ceremonial. We have already explored the stress this can awaken in people when we considered the introduction of liturgical dance to a tradition accustomed to a minimum of bodily action in worship.

The conflict between ceremonial and energetic uses of the body recurs again and again in the church. Here is a striking example of the phenomenon from the history of preaching. I have chosen this incident because it takes place in Great Britain, and because I often hear people talk about white European English-speaking culture as though it is a homogenous and coherent entity. The following bit of history shows the reality to be in fact much more pluralistic, especially when it comes to the use of the body in worship.

> An English traveler, B. H. Malkin, who happened to visit Merthyr (Wales) at about the time it was experiencing its first recorded revival in 1803, commented that, "Almost all the exclusively Welsh sects among the lower orders of the people have in truth degenerated into habits of the most pitiable lunacy in their devotion." Most English observers constantly highlighted the over-indulgence of Welsh revivals and cited as evidence the common practice of "jumping." Welsh preachers, though, defended such charges with vigour. The celebrated Baptist preacher Christmas Evans, for example, maintained that this emotion and the sympathy of feeling which existed between the preacher and his congregation was the force that had sent the Gospel, "...into every nook of the mountains of Wales, as well as into the cities, towns and villages; while in England, with all the advantages of education, the Gospel, in a manner is hid in the corner...Common preaching will not do to rouse sluggish districts from the heavy slumber into which they are sunk. Indeed, formal prayers and lifeless sermons are like bulwarks raised against these things in England."[29]

Note the sharp conflict of judgment in this story. The British observer of the Welsh revivals considers the dramatic use of the body an indication that the participants have "degenerated into habits of the most pitiable lunacy in their devotion." But the Welsh preacher is no less damning of his critic's ways, describing them as "bulwarks raised against" spiritual vitality.

These differences about the use of the body are planted so deeply within us that even when our intention is to be accepting of others, it remains difficult to refrain from judgment about somatic idioms that are different from our own. For example, Brenda Eatman Aghahowa has written a book that expresses a gracious spirit rooted in keen theological observation and principle. "All the well-intentioned talk in certain circles of the body of Christ about the need for ecumenical cooperation around issues of justice and peace can be nullified by the lack of tolerance and understanding between proponents of either formal or charismatic worship."[30] Her terms "formal" and "charismatic" include the differences between the ceremonial and energetic uses of the body.

As long as she remains at the level of principle and concept, Aghahowa manages to show the inclusive, cross-cultural perspective for which our world is desperate. But when she moves into an assessment of a somatic idiom that is different from her own, she makes judgments that are as severe as those that passed between the British observer and the Welsh preacher in the nineteenth century. Evaluating a service whose somatic idiom is clearly ceremonial, Aghahowa concludes that the Statue of Liberty, "a mere concrete monument, received more exuberant praise and cheering in one weekend than Jesus Christ, Savior of the world, receives in a lifetime at many churches—a sad indictment."[31] Yet faithful souls whose approach to God is ceremonial may be every bit as charismatic—that is, filled with the charism of the Spirit—as worshipers whose somatic idiom is energetically expressive. To judge ceremonial behavior as a "sad indictment" is the kind of "liturgical imperialism" that the author rightly decries when she writes about "the imposition of Euro-American worship preferences on Christians of African or other descent."[32]

If someone as thoughtful and gracious as Aghahowa stumbles when it comes to understanding a somatic idiom different from her own, then it is a sign of how deeply conflicted these matters can become when we attempt to reach across our cultural divisions. I do not know if it will ever be possible to bring a sense of being at ease with a somatic idiom that radically differs from the one that from childhood was implanted in our blood and our bone. Some individuals and some congregations may achieve this, but it is a very demanding transformation, and we may sometimes think we have accomplished it when we have not.

I remember, for example, an incident related by a Native American colleague. A group of white women visited his nation during a ceremonial dance. After watching for a while, they stood up and joined in the dance. They tried imitating the movements that they had observed, but they were unable to master the gestures and movements that belonged to those who had spent their lives immersed in this particular somatic idiom. The white women meant to affirm the dance through their participation, but their inadequate performance had just the opposite affect among the Native Americans.

Three Principles for Reaching across Different Somatic Idioms

If we want to understand and affirm a somatic idiom that is different from our own, I believe we must start by acknowledging at least three things:

- how and where our particular somatic idiom was formed, with attention to the memories that were especially formative in our upbringing
- the somatic idiom often lies deeper than words and concepts, and the best intentioned thought and the most rational analysis may not overcome the body's resistance to new postures and gestures
- the theological meaning we associate with a particular somatic idiom is not the same for all cultures.

The first principle gives people the freedom to begin with what has shaped them and why they use their bodies the way they do. This allows for people to be descriptive and autobiographical. It raises their consciousness so that they no longer assume that their particular use of the body is "natural." Instead, they come to appreciate that it is something acquired from childhood on, that it is part of the identity that the culture has planted in them.

The second principle frees us to acknowledge the inner conflict that we may feel between what we think with our heads and what we feel in our bones. In the story of the women preaching students, one of the most important advances was when they were able to be honest about their own internal resistance to doing what they knew they were called to do.

The third principle is perhaps the most difficult, for we often describe the actions of worship and preaching as being holy, sacramental, sacred, blessed, and handed on to us through scripture and tradition. The action of the body and the meaning flow together, and our theology reinforces their interfusion. For example, the values of moderation and reserve as expressed through the ceremonial of the early church were taken to be an expression of the character of the Divine: "God-like immobility or the absence of emotion was preferred to the 'undisciplined' flexing of the body. Immobility symbolized perfection. God is the unmoved mover."[33] For those who believe this about God, dramatic and energetic gestures awaken a feeling that the holy has been violated, the Divine mocked and devalued.

But how utterly different things appear when an energetic use of the body is interfused with an understanding that the universe and its Creator are in constant motion. For example, in many African cultures,

> The rhythm of the dance puts one in tune with the original rhythm of the universe as interpreted by ancestral memory. The sound of the human voice singing, and especially the sound of the drum, provokes the flexing of the body, puts the community and individuals in motion, to realize themselves in relationship. Life tends towards its aim (its completion) in the rhythmic *motion towards*. The human community, and the individual person, is in motion towards completion, in motion towards the other. The "motion towards," or relatedness, is the most fundamental element in the social definition of person and community.[34]

For people who hold these beliefs, the failure to move is a failure to express the holy, a failure to be in touch with the animating energy of their Creator.

Implications of a Shifting Somatic Idiom for Worship and Preaching

Over the last twenty-five years, I have been leading conferences for mainline churches in preaching and worship. During that time, I have encountered certain recurring themes about the use of the body in worship and preaching that indicate we are living in a time when the somatic idiom of many churches is changing. I have not done a scientific poll of these changes, but I have traveled widely, and the churches involved range from small rural congregations to suburban and city churches of every size.

The first is my observation that many preachers have stepped out of the pulpit to deliver their sermons. Although sometimes congregations resist this move, many of them welcome or even ask for the change. Sometimes it is the preacher who resists. But once preachers do leave the pulpit, there are important questions about how they will use their bodies:

- Will they walk among the congregation?
- Will they stand in the chancel or at center stage?
- Will they plant their feet firmly and keep still?
- Will they adopt different postures appropriate to what they are saying?
- Will they be holding a manuscript or index cards with an outline or a Bible? How will they gesture?

No matter how these questions are answered, preachers report to me that they get a wide range of intense responses to what they *do*, not just to what they say, once they have left the pulpit. Sometimes they are baffled by how to respond. A good place to begin is by understanding the somatic idiom of the person responding. For example, older members of a church, who grew up in a somatic culture where they were taught to "be still when you talk," may find it difficult to accept the increased kinetic energy that usually accompanies stepping out of the pulpit. Others who like significant distance between themselves and a speaker may feel threatened by someone who walks toward them while preaching. The concept of somatic idiom can help preachers understand the basis of such reactions, and it can also make preachers aware of their own somatic idiom. They will become more attentive to how the use of their bodies affects the way the congregation receives and processes their sermon.

My second observation is the number of hearing people who appreciate having someone sign the service and sermon for those who are hearing impaired or deaf. Many hearing people have told me they no longer watch the preacher, but the one who is signing, because even though they do not know sign language, the gestures add a greater depth of meaning to the spoken word. Their affirmation of sign language suggests how important bodily expression is to preaching. This does not mean that preachers ought to adopt forced gestures and dramatic postures that do not flow from them. But it does suggest that preachers need to find ways to achieve the maximum freedom of expressive movement that the somatic idiom of their congregation permits.

Finally, I have been struck by the rapidly increasing amount of mime and liturgical movement that I find in churches, as well as the use of screens to project hymns and songs so that people can look up and not be so tied to the page of a hymnal. There is clearly some hunger for a freer somatic idiom in these congregations, while at the same time there are many who find increased movement in worship awkward.

When there is conflict over somatic idiom in a church, how will people negotiate the differences? Drawing on the three principles I name in the preceding section of this chapter, pastors can help the parties develop a capacity to honor, if not to participate, in another culture's somatic idiom and to understand that the plurality of bodily expression is a witness to the multiplicity of ways in which the Spirit is manifest through preaching and worship. Perhaps God has allowed for so many different somatic idioms in order to remind us that God is not captured or bound to a single culture's mode of bodily expression. We give thanks for whatever repertoire of gesture and posture opens us to the divine presence. Yet at the same time we realize that the Creator of all things is equally pleased by stillness or motion, by moderation or excess, by ceremony or spontaneity, provided it is offered from the heart as an act of genuine worship and praise.

5

LANGUAGE

The Limits of Language

Several years ago a colleague, Professor Jane Smith, invited me to be a guest lecturer in her course "Varieties of Human Religiousness." Her goal was to help theological students, many of them future pastors, understand what it means to live and minister in a religiously pluralistic world. Professor Smith asked that I reflect on the course readings from my perspective as an ordained Christian minister and a professor of preaching and worship. The books and articles contained vivid descriptions of rituals in which few of us had ever participated.

Before discussing the readings, I went to the board and wrote down a single sentence: "God has set us free. Hallelujah! Hallelujah!" I asked that the students who had just arrived on campus for this particular class raise their hands. I then invited them to pretend that they were archeologists who five hundred years from now discover the words I had written on the board. What might they say in interpreting this verbal artifact from half a millennium earlier? Many keen observations followed about the nature and meaning of the sentence: how it opened with a theological claim and then broke into a ritual form of celebration, how the repeated "Hallelujahs" gave it a poetic sound and suggested energy and pulse. Typical of theological students and the culture of seminary education, the responses revealed a sophisticated level of articulation.

Then I asked the students who had been in chapel earlier that morning what they would say about the words. They immediately pointed out that we had sung the words over and over to the playing of six African drums while a gifted song leader led us in the melody, using a call-and-response pattern that enabled us to echo the variations that he kept adding to the music. The tempo had gradually accelerated, and the dynamic level had grown louder and louder. People had begun clapping, swaying, dancing, and adding their own variations. The singing of that song was an exuberant, joyful celebration. People came out of the chapel embracing one another, some laughing, some continuing to sing the words as they went down the stairs. The students who reported this to their classmates ended with, "You had to be there."

I observed to the class: A lot of theological study lacks the quality of being there. Fixated on language, there is a failure to place texts in their embodied, vocalized, material setting. This does *not* mean that words do not matter. If we had been asked to sing, "God has enslaved us" instead of "God has set us free," we would have choked on the words, and all the drumming in the world would not have evoked the rhapsodic response that had filled the chapel. Language matters. It matters mightily, but anytime we turn to language in understanding the interrelationship of preaching, worship, and culture, we need to alert ourselves to the distortions that occur when we study language free of the context that produced it and in which it is used. That is why I am turning to the consideration of language only after first exploring the visual, oral, and bodily differences between cultures. The organization of this book is not idiosyncratic, but flows from a general principle that is increasingly taking root among theological and literary disciplines: "For many scholars, texts and beliefs no longer float free, to be interpreted only in relation to other texts and ideas, but are understandable only within the concrete particularities of historical existence. Thus, the dominance of exegetical, philological, and hermeneutical methods is yielding to social, cultural, and political analysis."[1]

We have already seen this scholarly principle in action when we read the psalms in light of the iconography of the ancient Near East. Pictures of people dancing, weeping, and bowing gave a force to the words that language alone does not carry. However, recognizing the material context in which words are used does not settle all of our conflicts over language. Far from being a neutral medium, language itself turns out to be as culturally contested as are the use of eye, ear, and body.

Rhetorical Cultures

People's linguistic worlds are often strikingly different, even when they speak the same language (e.g., English, Spanish, Chinese). Rhetoric—the verbal strategy of a speaker or writer—varies with many factors, including race, gender, class, and geographic location. Conversation in the stands at a wrestling match is not the same as it is at a cocktail party in the country club. Human beings live in different rhetorical cultures. A rhetorical culture is a group's shared understanding of how language is to be used in particular acts of speech.

Conflicts between rhetorical cultures often erupt when we talk about preaching and worship. Most churches and regular attendees have clear ideas about how preachers should preach. For some, a sermon ought to proceed with clear logic and have a single shining point. For others, it should be an exposition of a biblical passage. Still others may expect an unfolding narrative structure rather than a rational progression of ideas.

Different rhetorical cultures also operate with different rubrics for the style of language, whether it ought to be high-toned, colloquial, or resonant with King Jamesian expressions and cadences.

There are even different rubrics for how preachers inflect what they say. In some rhetorical cultures, the preacher speaks with a minimum variation in vocal dynamics. In others, the preacher starts low and relaxed, then builds in tempo and dynamic level. In still others, the preacher becomes softer and softer to indicate the sacred significance of what is said.

When we turn to the liturgy itself, the conflicts are as intense as they are about preaching. There are people who insist on the historic language of their tradition without modification. Others require more contemporary, colloquial speech or language that is purified of any exclusionary or prejudicial bias. Some favor hymn texts that show theological development, poetically expressed as the poem moves from stanza to stanza. Others are eager to abandon such literary sophistication in favor of much simpler praise choruses that depend on verbal repetition.

Leonora Tubbs Tisdale gives a vivid account of how these varied rhetorical expectations affected her early ministry. She and her husband were serving in a parish of four congregations. They quickly discovered that sermons that worked well in one congregation failed in another.[2] Over the years I have had pastors tell me a similar story again and again. It goes like this: "I had preached a particular sermon in my last congregation, and people afterwards told me it was the best I ever preached. Then I moved and preached it in my new setting, and it flopped." Although there are multiple ways to interpret what happened, one strong possibility is that there was a difference in the rhetorical cultures of the two congregations.

Preaching as a Rhetorical Balancing Act

Even within the same rhetorical culture there are different rules for different acts of speech. Intimate conversation between two close friends, for example, will generally have different rules from those that govern preaching a sermon. How effective we are in any rhetorical culture depends on balancing the integrity of our self-expression with the assumed rubrics of the community we address. "Language is not a congeries of idiolects but something we construct together, in society, the individual both inheriting it and actively collaborating with others to develop it."[3]

This dynamic of inheriting yet developing language captures a struggle that every effective preacher knows: How do I preach so that what I say can be received, while at the same time the sermon allows in fresh understanding the living Spirit, the revealing word of God? This is a question about rhetorical culture that is implicitly present in a preacher's struggle to communicate effectively with a congregation. Experienced preachers come to realize that: "Both the communal and the individual emphases can be carried to extremes, and the extremity is loneliness. One can be lonely in the totalitarian crowd, in which no difference is perceived or tolerated; and one can be lonely in the difference or uniqueness of individuality in which community is repudiated."[4]

Rhetorical balancing acts become especially complex when a culture is incapable of receiving and honoring the rhetoric of certain groups that are trying to gain a hearing. It is difficult for them to get their message across because it does not fit within the "established regimes of thought."[5] Instead of being heard, they receive what Teresa Fry Brown terms "derisive communicative treatment" as manifest, for example, in the "historical ignoring or conspiratorial stifling of the existence and relevancy of the language and literature of black women."[6] When this happens, it takes courage and hope to believe in

the possibility that there is a word, that there are so many words, awaiting woman speech. And perhaps there is a word

that has not yet come to sound—a word that once we begin
to speak will round out and create deeper experience for us
and put us in touch with sources of power, energy of which
we are just beginning to become aware.[7]

The Post-Christian Clash of Rhetorical Cultures

One way to describe the current theological situation of the church
is to say that we are involved in a clash of rhetorical cultures:

- cultures that represent the historically powerful, "the established regimes of thought"
- cultures that represent the historically suppressed or ignored
- cultures that represent new possibilities in the process of emerging.

Two terms that are used to characterize this situation are *postmodern*
and *post-Christian*. I hear them in conversation with colleagues and
find them in my general reading. The terms are not precisely
synonymous, but both point to the demise of a once-coherent
rhetorical culture that was rooted in the Bible and that extended into
the general discourse of the whole society.

Within the church there is a wide spectrum of response to this
post-Christian reality. Some abhor it; some welcome it; and the
differences between the groups often result in pitched battles over
the language of preaching and prayer. There are charges and
countercharges about who is being "biblical" and who is not. Because
the Bible is so central to the church's preaching and prayer, and
because it figures prominently in the church's debates about how to
respond to a post-Christian world, we need to clarify our
understanding of the rhetorical character of the Bible. Without such
understanding, our efforts to live faithfully amidst a variety of
rhetorical cultures will fail.

Some biblical authors draw from sources outside of their own
rhetorical culture, often using their images and metaphors or adapting
their forms of argument and persuasion. Others reinterpret earlier
writers to address new situations and new issues. Editors interweave
conflicting versions of the same story. Viewed from this literary-
historical angle, the Bible is a record of multiple rhetorical cultures
sometimes in dialogue, sometimes in conflict, sometimes transforming
each other.[8]

The Bible, then, provides a model for how faith finds multiple
forms of expression. Instead of drawing on the Bible solely for content,
we examine the Bible for its paradigmatic wisdom, for the way it

demonstrates how God's *logos* is revealed through a multiplicity of rhetorical cultures. Our focus in reading the Bible is not trained exclusively on the denotative meaning of the words, but also on the patterns of interaction between biblical authors and their surrounding cultures.

What do those patterns suggest about how faith is to find expression in a post-Christian world?

A good place to begin is to trace the history of the word *Christian,* because the term post-Christian presupposes that there was an earlier era that was *Christian.* We may all bring a different set of meanings to the term *post-Christian* unless we share some common understanding of the varied meanings and associations that have clustered around the word *Christian* over the last two thousand years.

The Word *Christian*: From Minority Status to Imperial Grandeur

The word *Christian* appears only three times in the Bible, twice in Acts and once in 1 Peter.[9] Acts 11:26b reads: "It was in Antioch that the disciples were first called 'Christians.'" Luke, the author of Acts, leaves it at that. His tone is nearly parenthetical. We might expect that Luke would make some theological comment about this naming the followers of Jesus "Christians." Luke's standard practice is to offer a theological interpretation of nearly every event he reports. For example, in this same chapter, Luke invokes the Holy Spirit to justify fellowship with Gentiles (11:15–17), to confirm the authority of the ministry of Barnabas (11:24), and to explain the prophetic powers of Agabus, who predicts a coming famine (11:28). But Luke does nothing like this in reporting the first use of the word *Christian.* He eschews any theological reflection on the word. Luke does not even identify who coined the term, although it appears from the text that outsiders dubbed the disciples "Christians," possibly to distinguish them from other Jews, who required that Gentile converts be circumcised.

We may never know who first came up with the term *Christian,* but we do know this about them: They lived in a cosmopolitan city that was home to many different rhetorical cultures. Located on the Orontes River in the northwestern corner of the Roman province of Syria, Antioch was "the third largest city of the empire, a center of Greek culture, and a commercial hub…[Antioch was characterized by] a prosperous urban culture, a Judaism used to contacts with Gentiles, an intellectual and religious milieu open to many currents, interest in mystery cults, fine roads and lines of communication."[10]

At the time the word *Christian* was coined, the religious scene in Antioch was "a complex picture of developing religions, sometimes in conflict with each other, sometimes overlapping, sometimes merging at the edges. The dispersal of Christians northward from Jerusalem after the martyrdom of Stephen carried the Christian gospel into this complex and unstable setting."[11]

It was, then, in a religiously pluralistic culture that the word *Christian* was first spoken. The term helped distinguish one religious group from the many others that thrived in the city of Antioch. *Christian* did not originally describe anything so vast or momentous as an era in history or a worldview shared by many nations and peoples.

Over the centuries *Christian* became a word of much greater dimensions. What once had been a label for a fledgling new religious movement took on weighty rhetorical significance. The *Oxford English Dictionary* gives a number of literary citations demonstrating how *Christian* came to be used to distinguish between brute beasts and human beings. Depending on one's theology and social location, the word *Christian* might evoke a certain grandeur, as in the phrases: "A Christian nation," "Christian values," "The Christian era."

If these are the associations and connotations that we bring to the word *Christian,* then the phrase "post-Christian era" may indicate for us a loss of significance. We may feel that the march of history has robbed us of an identity that the world used to value and honor.

Fear of living in a "post-Christian era" is one of the things I discovered online. When I entered the phrase "post-Christian era," my internet explorer returned 147,255 entries! To the extent that virtual reality maps the topography of contemporary consciousness, there is a great deal of interest in our post-Christian era. It is also apparent that the term *post-Christian* functions in extremely different ways, depending on the rhetorical culture of the Web site.

Dipping in and out of the list of 147,255 entries, I found a few sites tracing intellectual developments in academic theology, but I more often came across fear and condemnation of our entering a post-Christian era. These Internet sites presuppose what the word *Christian* came to mean *after* the church had become a major social institution, after its rituals, symbols, and theology had profoundly shaped Europe and the lands that Europe settled and colonized.

The Formative Function of a Rhetorical Culture

The authors of many Web sites find the term *post-Christian* frightening because it signifies to them the loss of a rhetorical culture that was shaped and sustained by the Bible and by the theological idiom of the church. They were at home in that culture. They knew how to talk its talk, how to negotiate their way through the struggles of life by drawing on its rubrics of communication. The diminishment of that rhetorical culture is to them a diminishment of themselves, their sense of power and respect. To such believers, *post-Christian* implies a rejection of biblical faith.

Although I have strong reservations about these Web sites, especially their tendency to protect "the established regimes of thought," I believe it is unfair to dismiss them entirely out of hand. They raise important questions about what our current mass culture consumes intellectually, emotionally, and spiritually.

Reading these sites makes me think of the dietary mantra "You are what you eat." Many years ago I was visiting a grade school that was celebrating National Nutrition Week. A teacher had placed this phrase across the top of a bulletin board. Beneath the words was the artwork of first and second graders. A man whose arms and legs were bananas was eating a banana. A woman whose head and torso were oranges was eating an orange. A man whose head was the head of a cow was eating a hamburger.

"You are what you eat." The children had taken the slogan literally, and the resulting pictures struck me at first as bizarre and humorous.

But now, reading the Web sites that condemn the advent of a post-Christian world, I see how the children's literal minds captured a truth that may elude our more sophisticated thought, a truth that feeds the authors of those fearful Web sites: We are what we eat; we become what we consume. Looking at the greed, violence, and gratuitous sex that stream from the electronic media, believers have good reason to resist the spiritual diet of a post-Christian consumer society.

The formation of our character, the formation of our understanding of life, the formation of our patterns of response to the world—all of these depend on what we consume. One of the functions of a rhetorical culture is to provide a diet of healthy language that will strengthen us for the challenges of living. Our ancient forbears in the faith gave eloquent witness to this essential truth. Consider the opening of Psalm 1:

> Happy are those
>   who do not follow the advice of the wicked,
>   or take the path that sinners tread,
>   or sit in the seat of scoffers;

but their delight is in the law of the LORD,
    and on his law they meditate day and night.
They are like trees
    planted by streams of water,
which yield their fruit in its season,
    and their leaves do not wither.
In all that they do, they prosper. (Ps. 1:1–3)

To meditate on the law day and night is to immerse ourselves in the rhetorical culture of the ancient Hebrews, thus making a steady diet of a good and gracious gift from God.

The Biblical Interfusion of Different Rhetorical Cultures

The psalm, however, is not committed exclusively to the rhetorical culture of the Hebrews. Othmar Keel believes the poet derived the image of the tree from Egypt, particularly from Egyptian wisdom literature. The willingness of the Hebrews to borrow from surrounding cultures suggests that: "Israel did not live in isolation. It engaged in an active intellectual exchange with the world around it. Not infrequently, this posed a catastrophic threat to Israel's particularity. However, it also permitted Israel's experiences and conceptions of God to be rounded out by those of neighboring peoples."[12]

The willingness of the Hebrews to round out their understanding of God by borrowing from others has implications for the shaping of the church's rhetorical culture in a post-Christian world. It suggests that to be biblical is to be in relationship with the surrounding culture and even willing to draw on its images and literature to the extent that they enrich, expand, and deepen our relationship to God.

When we turn to the early church, we discover a continuing interfusion between the rhetorical cultures of the community of faith and the surrounding world. New Testament authors often employed language and images from the pluralistic societies in which they lived.

We have already traced how the term *Christian* arose in a cosmopolitan, pluralistic city that was a center of commerce and communication and whose religious life has been characterized as "complex and unstable." When the followers of Jesus were first termed "Christian," they lived in a society that knew the strain and stress of conflicting cultures and value systems. We hear the rumble of those conflicts throughout the New Testament. Consider, for example, how much ink the apostle Paul spends trying to get people from different backgrounds to live together as the body of Christ!

Our forbears in the faith made a witness to Christ amidst intercultural complexity. The age in which they ministered was not unlike our own. The ethos of the first-century church was in many ways closer to our post-Christian era than when the church was at the height of its power and grander, more imperial meanings clustered around the word *Christian.*

If we want to develop a rhetorical culture for the church in a post-Christian world, then we study the Bible not only for its content but also for the linguistic strategies of its authors. Like us, those ancient writers had to find a way of expressing their faith that was true to their belief yet accessible to those who thought and expressed themselves through many different idioms. Consider, for example, the cosmological language used in Colossians to describe Christ as

> the image of the invisible God,
> the firstborn of all creation;
> for in him all things in heaven and on earth were
>   created,
> things visible and invisible,
> whether thrones or dominions or rulers or powers–
> all things have been created through him and for him.
> He himself is before all things,
> and in him all things hold together.
> He is the head of the body, the church;
> he is the beginning, the firstborn from the dead,
> so that he might come to have first place in
>   everything.
> For in him all the fullness of God was pleased to dwell,
> and through him God was pleased to reconcile to
>   himself all things,
> whether on earth or in heaven,
>   by making peace through the blood of his cross.
>   (Col. 1:15–20)

Colossae, like Antioch, was a pluralistic city, a home to many different religions and, therefore, to many different rhetorical cultures. Raymond Brown observes that Colossae was located in an area where "religious observances reflected a mixture of native Phrygian cults, Eastern imports (Isis, Mithras), Greco-Roman deities, and Judaism with its insistence on one God."[13] The church in Colossae, like our post-Christian era, knew the tension of multiple religious and philosophical views.

The verses I have quoted are an early Christian hymn, possibly modified to fit the writer's argument more cogently.[14] Because hymns are one of the most important ways that worshiping communities inculcate their understanding of faith, the passage gives us access to the character of the rhetorical culture of early Christian worship. The writer of the letter grants substantial authority to the hymn. He appeals to it as the basis of his theological admonitions to the Colossians.

The language of the hymn blends Greek and Hebraic cultures. The descriptions of God and Christ resonate with overtones from Hellenistic writings, while the role of Christ in creation echoes claims about Wisdom in the Book of Proverbs. The cultural confluence of the hymn is significant: It tells us that while our ancestors drew their unique identity from Christ, they were not shy about drawing from the idiom of other religions to express their faith. When the materials of the surrounding rhetorical culture enriched the expression of belief, our ancestors were willing to interfuse them in Christian worship, even into their hymns.

The author of the hymn employs language in a way that simultaneously affirms and transforms the rhetorical culture of the Colossians. After the poetic splendor of the hymn's opening verses, the poem ends with "making peace through the blood of his cross." The blood and the cross reframe the eloquent flourishes that begin the hymn so as to produce a new rhetorical culture, one that blends together Hellenistic and Semitic elements.

The poetic synthesis of splendor and blood results in an extraordinary theological vision that spans from the sublimity of the One who has created us to the brutality of human violence. The imaginative daring of the poet, the willingness to interfuse two different rhetorical cultures, vitalizes the witness to Christ.

If the Colossian hymn had only the grandeur of God and "no blood of [Christ's] cross," then belief might devolve into escapism: We would be related to a sublime deity that has no interest in our violent, bleeding world. Or if the Colossian hymn had only the blood and no grandeur, then belief might devolve into despair. We would be related to a God who has no power to lift our vision beyond the brutal life we suffer here and now.

But this hymn has both splendor and blood, and it locates their interconnection in the nature of God and God's action in Christ. Only by a vision this expansive can we face the truth of our human situation, both its devastation and its hope. The vision was born in a willingness to interfuse two different rhetorical cultures in one unified witness to God's creative and redemptive work.

We see this same pattern replicated in Paul's letter to the Philippians. Although some scholars question the textual integrity of the epistle and consider it to be assembled out of several different communications from the apostle, I am intrigued that Philippians provides instructions for our spiritual formation that draw on the rhetorical cultures of the fledgling church's liturgical life and philosophical Greek thought. The first of these is present in the famous kenotic hymn (hymn of self-emptying):

> Let the same mind be in you that was in Christ Jesus,
>   who, though he was in the form of God,
>   did not regard equality with God
>   as something to be exploited,
>   but emptied himself,
>   taking the form of a slave,
>   being born in human likeness. (Phil. 2:5–7a)

Once again, as in the case of Colossians, the incorporation of a hymn into a homiletical epistle gives us a sense of the rhetorical culture of the early church, what kinds of language were shaping the religious imagination of Christian worshipers. Paul uses the hymn to contrast the mind of Christ with what he describes as "a crooked and perverse generation" (Phil. 2:15). If we were to read only this chapter of the letter, we might decide that expressing the Christian faith requires that believers be exclusively immersed in the church's rhetorical culture without ever drawing on other forms of thought and expression.

But in the fourth chapter of the epistle the apostle turns to classical Greek thought as he offers the Philippians further guidance about their spiritual formation: "Finally, beloved, whatever is true, whatever is honorable, whatever is just, whatever is pure, whatever is pleasing, whatever is commendable, if there is any excellence and if there is anything worthy of praise, think about these things" (Phil. 4:8). F. W. Beare notes the following:

> The striking feature about the injunction...is that Paul here sanctifies, as it were, the generally accepted virtues of pagan morality. None of the words which he uses is specifically Christian; some of them are not found elsewhere in the New Testament...It follows that Paul had come to recognize that there was a genuine capacity for moral discernment in the pagan society around him, and that things which were counted honourable by good men everywhere were in fact

worthy of honour, worthy to be cultivated by a Christian believer.[15]

Rhetorical Interfusion Leads to a More Adequate Theology

Fred B. Craddock, in a more homiletical commentary on the same text from Philippians, observes:

> Outside the circles of Jewish and Christian faith are those men and women whose conduct and relationships exhibit qualities enjoined upon those within those circles. How can persons nurtured in philosophies and religions broadly classed as pagan embody virtues appropriate to believers in God and Jesus Christ? The fact that this was and still is an undeniable fact has been to some Christians a strange embarrassment rather than a condition to be celebrated. The church that takes a rigid over-against-the world posture is now and again forced to go in search of a more adequate theology.[16]

Craddock's reflection on the implications of Paul's appeal to pagan thought makes clear that the interfusion of different rhetorical cultures involves far more than literary or oratorical technique. Such interfusion leads us into profound theological concerns about the relationship of language to the reality of God, goodness, truth, justice, and love. It is significant that Craddock works his way toward these concerns not by relying on language alone but by appealing to the quality of "conduct and relationships" outside the circle of Christianity. "Conduct and relationships" are dimensions of human life that are not confined to language alone. By blending Christian idiom with pagan philosophical discourse, Paul reveals that the realities to which the gospel point are greater than can be caught in any single rhetorical culture. The result is to provide the Philippians with what Craddock terms "a more adequate theology."

If we apply our earlier principle that we read the Bible not only for content but for its paradigmatic wisdom, then Colossians and Philippians suggest to us patterns for developing a more adequate theology for our pluralistic post-Christian era. Theological adequacy will involve empowering people to respond to other cultures without falling into the extreme patterns of total rejection or faithless acquiescence.

Philippians and Colossians reveal that interfusing rhetorical cultures in a manner that has integrity requires at least two things:

- deep rooting in our own faith tradition
- openness to the revelation of goodness and truth wherever they may be found and whatever idiom they may bear.

As Vatican II announced in the *Constitution on the Church in the Modern World*: "It is the task of the Church to uncover, cherish, and ennoble all that is true, good, and beautiful in the human community."[17] Our need to live these words became forcefully apparent in the weeks following September 11, 2001. People of good will from multiple religious traditions came together to claim "what is true, good, and beautiful in the human community," and not just in their own rhetorical culture.

I recall attending an interreligious worship service after the attack on the World Trade Center. I thought back to my colleague's class, "Varieties of Human Religiousness." Her goal had been to help theological students, many of them future pastors, understand what it means to live and minister in a religiously pluralistic world. Now attending this interreligious service, I knew the wisdom of what she had been trying to teach us. Muslims, Jews, Buddhists, Christians, and Hindus gathered as one. Each group prayed, meditated, sang, chanted, reflected, or invited us to silence according to the practice of their tradition. They did not modify their rhetorical cultures, but each used the language that helped them to negotiate their way through grief and rage toward some sense of meaning and hope.

I remember often being moved and sometimes baffled by practices and language that do not shape my daily prayer. I also remember realizing that we who are Christian in a post-Christian era will not be faithful to the living Spirit of God unless we are open to all that is "true, good, and beautiful in the human community," even when it finds expression in a rhetorical culture that is utterly unlike our own. To live this way does not mean abandoning the particularity of our Christian belief and practices. The strength of that interreligious service lay in the fact that people were faithful to their traditions. If they had abandoned their distinctive rhetorical cultures and had reduced the service to interreligious pudding, the whole event would have seemed shallow, lacking integrity and power.

The interreligious service confirmed a principle that a devout Jewish colleague and I have discovered through many years of conversation: namely, that we are most helpful to each other when we boldly claim our beliefs. Our mutual understanding and enrichment are directly proportional to the depth and clarity of our particular commitments, to our fluency in the rhetorical cultures that have nurtured the expression and understanding of our faith.

Perhaps this is why the psalmist was able to adapt the tree imagery from Egyptian wisdom literature: He was so centered in the Torah and in God that he was unthreatened by the surrounding culture. He was thereby free to enrich his faith with what was good and true in another's. He was free to deepen and expand the expression of his own prayer and devotion by drawing from sources whose origins lay beyond his native rhetorical culture.

And perhaps this is why the author of Colossians and Paul the apostle were able to draw freely from pagan and philosophical idioms. The author of Colossians was so convinced that the blood and cross were the source of his salvation that he was glad to adapt the poetic splendor of Greek cosmological language, and Paul was so filled with the mind of Christ that it pointed him to see the wisdom of asking people to think on whatever was excellent. The sign that people possess a deep and secure faith is their openness to expressions of belief that represent rhetorical cultures different from their own. Instead of perceiving a threat, they seek to honor all that is "true, good, and beautiful in the human community."

Expanding Our Metaphors for the Bible

The capacity of Christians to welcome the wisdom of other rhetorical cultures is a gift from the Bible itself, from the character of its witness: "The fountain-head of the power of the Bible in literature lies in its nearness to the very springs and sources of human life—life taken seriously, earnestly, intensely; life in its broadest meaning, including the inward as well as the outward; life interpreted in its relation to universal laws and eternal values."[18]

If the Bible embodies "nearness to the very springs and sources of human life," how do we account for the fact that some Christians use the Bible to exclude the church's consideration of what is true, good, and beautiful in the life of other cultures? There are many ways we could answer the question, including an appeal to proof texts, but I think a much more fruitful approach is to consider the primary metaphors by which we interpret the Bible as a symbol of faith.

The single most common metaphor is that the Bible is a book, the church's holy book. Depending on our tradition, the Bible may be carried into service during the procession, or it may be printed as a giant-sized volume that sits permanently on the pulpit or communion table/altar. Its physical presence as a single-bound volume reinforces an overarching theological construction that shapes our understanding of the unity and interrelationship of the scriptures. The Bible is one of those conceptual/poetic constellations that Sallie McFague, drawing on the work of Stephen Pepper, calls "root-metaphors."[19] We tend to work within the assumptions of our root-metaphors without questioning their implications. If our root-metaphor for the Bible is "book," then our interpretations may assume a consistency of viewpoint and doctrine that ignores or diminishes the variety of rhetorical cultures in the scriptures. No matter how well-trained we are in exegetical methods, the weight and mass of the root-metaphor tends to erase clashes in perspective and belief between various authors, between the variety of theologies that developed in different historical settings to speak to different needs.

There is an inconsistency in our root-metaphor: We refer to the "books" of the Bible rather than the "chapters" of the Bible. Nevertheless, our persistence in calling the Bible "The Book" or "The Good Book" or "The Church's Book" dims our awareness of the Bible as a collection of books. The root-metaphor swallows up the diversity.

"Library" as Root-metaphor

I cannot recall who first suggested to me that we begin to think of the Bible as a library rather than a book. It may have been my New Testament colleague, Dennis McDonald (formerly from Iliff, now teaching at Claremont), with whom I had many discussions about the Bible. But wherever the idea first came from, the metaphor of Bible as "library" rather than "book" has appeared in a number of different recent publications. Peter J. Gomes, in his effort to win thoughtful skeptics and peripheral believers to a serious reading of the Bible, observes that "the Bible is not a book but a library of books, written by many people in many forms over many years for many purposes."[20] He reinforces this distinction in his section on the construction of scripture "by stressing the fact that the Bible is not a book but a collection of books, in fact, a library of books."[21]

Ron Allen employs the same metaphor in cultivating how preachers can converse with the Bible: "The bible [*sic*] is a library of primal witnesses to the presence and purposes of God. I call it a library because, while its many books contain perspectives in common, the different bodies of literature within the bible have their own voices in the conversation, e.g., priestly writings, wisdom, literature, apocalypticism, Pauline and post-Pauline schools, Johannine community."[22]

Although these observations might seem rudimentary, I believe we have never adequately examined the hidden implications of these two different root-metaphors for the scriptures and how they lead us to be closed or open to the rhetorical cultures of different religious traditions. Consider how startling it would be to change the root-metaphor for the Bible. Think of the different evocations and associations we would touch off if we described the church as "the people of the Library," or if we referred to the Bible as the "Good Library" or the "Holy Library." These have an astonishingly different impact than the phrases "the people of the Book," the "Good Book," the "Holy Book." The shift in the root-metaphor opens up new possibilities for understanding the multiple rhetorical cultures of the scriptures. "Library" evokes different understandings of reality, perception, and authority than "Book."

Below is a chart of the most obvious contrasts between "Book" and "Library." There are, of course, many variations to books, including volumes that gather conflicting perspectives, just as there are different kinds of libraries serving different publics and purposes. But for now I am dealing with our more common expectations of books and libraries.

Book	Library
one author (editor)	multiple authors (editors)
one rhetorical culture	multiple rhetorical cultures
written at a particular point in time	written during multiple time periods
written with a particular perspective	written with multiple perspectives, including conflicting viewpoints
coherent values	multiple values
subject matter and style are representative of the author's period in history	multiple subject matters and styles are representative of different periods in history
knowledge and data are fixed in the text	knowledge and data are changing; new material contradicting older material is always coming in
authority (related to the word *author*) is clear	authority is multiple and is often in conflict; later authority may displace earlier authority
gives impression that one might master the text	gives impression that knowledge is too vast and complex to master
answers or "the whole story" is in the book	answers or "the whole story" is not in any one book but in the way the reader constructs understanding from multiple sources
has a clear ending; you can close book	has no clear ending; reader can always consider a different book

This list is in no way final and conclusive, but it is long enough to suggest what a significant difference it makes if we change our root-metaphor for the Bible from the "Good Book" to the "Good Library." I do not expect that church worship services will feature rolling the individual books of the Bible down the aisle on a library cart! Nevertheless, I hold up the image of the library as a way of counterbalancing the root-metaphor of the book. It is a complemental root-metaphor that could help open the church to rhetorical cultures different from its own. Without this counterbalancing root-metaphor, we stand in continual danger of forgetting that

> the Bible is not God, nor is it a substitute for God, and to treat it as if it were God or a surrogate of God is to treat it in the very way that it itself condemns over and over again. This first danger, giving to the Bible what belongs to God, while an understandable temptation on the part of the faithful, is nevertheless profoundly dangerous. In the name of God, and in the pursuit of good this danger will cause many to do much harm.[23]

Reframing the Ontology of the Bible

One of the great harms of bibliolatry (making the Bible an idol) is that it kills efforts at interreligious understanding. How will we who are Christian find ways to honor our rich biblical inheritance while at the same time entering into dialogue with traditions whose rhetorical cultures are entirely different from ours? The question compels us to address what James Sanders calls "the ontology of the Bible, its nature."[24] Given the centrality of the Bible to all our Christian traditions, it is not realistic to expect that the church will become open to serious and productive encounter with other rhetorical cultures unless we understand that the Bible embodies and grants authority to such efforts. We need new root-metaphors for the Bible that keep us ever mindful that many of its authors developed their idioms of faith through the interfusion of different rhetorical cultures.

Despite the differences between the book and library metaphors, they share one thing in common: printed words. Neither "book" nor "library" adequately communicates the dynamism of the Spirit that we experience when we read widely in the scriptures and find ourselves traveling among many different cultures. Henry Van Dyke, the poet who wrote one of the most beloved hymns in the English language, "Joyful, Joyful We Adore Thee," provides us with an entirely different kind of root-metaphor through a fable about the animating energies of the Bible. Van Dyke prefaces his fable with a general observation about books, how some are "dry and dusty, there is no juice in them; and many are soon exhausted, you would no more go back to them than to a squeezed orange; but some have in them an unfailing sap, both from the tree of knowledge and from the tree of life."[25] Here is Van Dyke's fable communicating how the Bible is a source of "unfailing sap."

> There was once an Eastern prince who was much enamoured of the art of gardening. He wished that all flowers delightful to the eye, and all fruits pleasant to the taste and good for food, should grow in his dominion, and that in growing the flowers should become more fair, the fruits more savoury and nourishing. With this thought in his mind and this desire in his heart, he found his way to the Ancient One, the Worker of Wonders who dwells in a secret place, and made known his request.
>
> "For the care of your gardens and your orchards," said the Ancient One, "I can do nothing, since that charge has been given to you and to your people. Nor will I send blossoming plants and fruiting trees of every kind to make your kingdom rich and beautiful as by magic, lest the honour of labour should be diminished, and the slow reward of patience despised, and even the living gifts bestowed upon you without toil should wither and die away. But this will I do: a single tree shall be brought to you from a far country by the hands of my servants, and you shall plant it in the midst of your land. In the body of that tree is the sap of life that was from the beginning; the leaves of it are full of healing; its flowers never fail, and its fruitage is the joy of every season. The roots of the tree shall go down to the springs of deep waters; and wherever its pollen is drifted by the wind or borne by the bees, the gardens shall put on new beauty; and wherever its seed is carried by the fowls of the air, the orchards shall yield a richer harvest. But the tree itself you guard and cherish and keep as I give it you, neither cutting anything away from it, nor grafting anything upon it; for the life of the tree is in all the branches and the other trees shall be glad because of it."
>
> As the Ancient One had spoken, so it came to pass. The land of that prince had great renown of fine flowers and

delicious fruits, ever unfolding in new colours and sweeter flavours the life that was shed among them by the tree of trees.[26]

To envision the Bible as a tree that taps deep springs, that flows with the sap of life, and that offers pollen and seed is to suggest the living, interactive character of the scriptures. The focus is not exclusively on the text itself, but rather on the life set loose by the text. Van Dyke makes this point in his gloss on the fable when he observes how the Bible has "given new impulse and form to the shaping imagination of [humanity], and begotten beauty in literature and the other arts."[27] Since the form of our imagination is largely a function of the rhetorical culture that has raised and shaped us, we can paraphrase van Dyke by saying that the Bible has given new impulse and form to the rhetorical cultures in which it has taken root.

Book, Library, Tree

When we imagine the Bible as all three—book, library, tree—then we simultaneously maintain the liturgical symbolism of a sacred volume (book), the reality of its multiple perspectives (library), and its interactive presence (tree). The expanded metaphorical range transforms our understanding of the ontology of the Bible. Instead of considering it a univocal authority, it becomes a paradigm or model for how God is known in and through a multiplicity of rhetorical cultures. Studying the Bible as a paradigm, and not simply a source of content, we become less scared by our post-Christian world. We begin to see that although the breakup of a hegemonic rhetorical culture leaves us "without any common grammar of thought wherewith we might give 'a candid kind to every thing,'" it also

> results in releasing us from the ossified formulas of the past, grants new opportunities for humbly and obediently hearkening to that—anciently spoken of as the Logos—which assembles and sustains the things and creatures of earth. Once again we are given a chance, as it were, to accord the initiative not to the engines of our own speculation but to the mysterious fecundity of What Is.[28]

A pluralism of rhetorical cultures thus helps us to avoid creating an idol out of our words. Before the "fecundity of What Is," we realize what we talking creatures so often forget: We can invoke but never capture the living Spirit of God with our net of words.

Implications of the Bible's Rhetorical Diversity:
Avoiding "Pericopeitis"

The tremendous popularity of the Common Lectionary across many Christian traditions has given birth to ecumenical groups of pastors meeting to prepare their sermons, to the reclaiming of passages that many preachers avoid, and to numerous high-quality homiletical and liturgical journals. But I have also noted a common homiletical malady that I have dubbed "pericopeitis," by which I mean getting stuck within the limits of an assigned text. There are, of course, occasions when an expository sermon from a single text is exactly what the Spirit calls us to preach. But if this is a preacher's only pattern, then the meta-message that the congregation receives over time is that the Bible is a collection of texts, each with equal authority but not necessarily related to some larger narrative or theological understanding. That is what I mean by "pericopeitis."

This is no small matter. Pericopeitis leads to a yet more serious illness: proof texting, the practice of citing an isolated biblical verse or passage as a theological absolute. Proof texting has been used through the centuries to enforce slavery, attack scientific discoveries, and deny women the vote and the use of anesthesia in childbirth–to name just a few egregious examples.

Here are three homiletical strategies that draw on scriptural diversity to cure pericopeitis and proof texting:

- Consult biblical scholarship to see if a passage is fusing together different rhetorical cultures. This is the strategy I used to examine Psalm 1, the Colossians hymn, and Philippians. Name the different rhetorics and their sources in the sermon so that people come to see how the biblical writers used materials from other cultures to enrich and strengthen their relationship to God.

- Point out how new theologies and new forms of religious language arise over the centuries in the scriptures. Help people to see that the Bible embraces a wide range of culture and practice.

- Stand back from your individual sermons and analyze whether your preaching leads people to appreciate the Bible not only as a book but as a library and tree. Your preaching over time needs to deepen their understanding of the Bible's astounding variety and how it most comes alive in interacting with us and our world.

If we follow these strategies, this post-Christian age may discover that the Bible illuminates the challenges of a pluralistic world, for the Bible reveals that God is known and honored through many cultures. The Bible frees us to be as faithfully creative in responding to our variegated world as the biblical authors were in responding to theirs. No longer frightened but delighted by the variety of God's world, we and the people to whom we preach will discover that post-Christian describes nothing more than a passing age. Post-Christian is not a description of ultimate truth. Post-Christian does not mean post-Christ. We have not left Christ behind; for Christ is here amidst our multiple cultures, and in Christ "all things hold together."

6

MEANING

A Mental Construction Framed by the Sensorium

Elochukwu E. Uzukwu tells, side by side, two stories that demonstrate how the same event can awaken different degrees of engagement and meaning in people, depending on the sensorium of their culture.

> **Story 1:** A Nigerian priest living in Germany took his guest (another Nigerian just arrived from the country) to hear the performance of a Beethoven symphony. While the German audience listened in rapt attention, the Nigerian guest was bored. He told his host, "Let's go!" The performance was hardly half-way through. There was no action. But of course there was action! The action of listening! Many Africans in Europe stop going to worship because the gesture of silent listening fails to communicate the sentiments of prayer.[1]

Understanding their different sensoria illuminates the reasons for the Germans' "rapt attention" and the Nigerian priest's being "bored." We do not have enough data to provide an exhaustive cultural analysis, but from what we do have, it is possible to fill out at least this much of the grid:

NIGERIAN AT BEETHOVEN CONCERT				
eye	**ear**	**body**	**language**	**meaning**
Expects to see a lot happening	Sonic idiom employs preeminently complex percussive rhythmic patterns	Expects the body to be used in energetic, highly visible ways, including the bodies of the audience	Not a dominant concern in this story	Sense that nothing is happening results in boredom
GERMAN AT BEETHOVEN CONCERT				
eye	**ear**	**body**	**language**	**meaning**
Expects to see only what is required for production of sound	Sonic idiom employs preeminently harmonization, inner voices, and melodic development and variation Rhythm is important but not preeminent	Expects the body to be used only to the extent that it is necessary to produce sound—e.g., bowing of string instruments, gestures from the conductor. Audience is to remain completely still and silent except for applause at the conclusion	Not a dominant concern in this story	Sense that a great deal of significance is happening results in rapt attention

Uzukwu balances his first story with a second one. This time it is the European who is baffled by an African performance of the mass.

Story 2: A French woman participated for the first time in an African mass to close the year in Rennes (France–18 May 1994). The choir selected French, Senegalese, Zairian, and

Congolese hymns. Guitars and drums accompanied the singing. But from the opening to the recessional hymn, the tapping of the hand and rhythmical swaying accompanied worship. As she explained to me after the mass, her initial reaction was shock. She never associated such gestures with prayer.[2]

AFRICAN LITURGISTS				
eye	**ear**	**body**	**language**	**meaning**
Expect to see energetic bodily engagement of participants	Expect some form of percussive sound throughout the mass	Expect kinetic motion: tapping, swaying, etc., throughout the service	Not significant as the story is told here	The mass is truly prayer because it embodies what it celebrates
FRENCH WOMAN				
eye	**ear**	**body**	**language**	**meaning**
Expects to see more reserved ceremonial worship	Expects some cessation of percussive sound and possibly periods of silence, or at least a more contemplative tone	Expects more reserved use of the body	Not significant as the story is told here	Shock. The mass is done in ways the woman "never associated with prayer."

Again, we do not have enough data for an exhaustive analysis, but there is enough to plot some of the outstanding differences between the French woman's sensorium and the Africans who led the mass.

Uzukwu records responses that range from "rapt attention" to "boredom" to "shock." Those are responses that most experienced pastors and worship leaders are familiar with, especially when they have attempted something new or when the congregation they serve has become more multicultural. When conflicts break out, a typical pattern is for people to debate "meaning." Thus, one group may speak of how "inspiring" or "beautiful" or "powerful" a service or sermon was, while others will say it was "boring" or "empty" or "meaningless." If the groups limit themselves to the discussion of meaning, they will seldom, if ever, find some way of understanding why they have responded in such entirely different ways. This is why it is essential to understand that "meaning" does not float in an ether of absolute ideas. Rather, meaning is the mental construction of purposeful relationships as framed by the sensorium of a particular culture.

Consider, for example, the Beethoven concert with the rapt German audience and the bored Nigerian priest. The German audience has been taught by their culture to expect a kind of sound that is organized according to certain principles of harmony, melody, rhythm, and orchestration. Some of them–I have observed this in concerts–will even close their eyes so as to be able to give themselves completely to the sound. They cannot take in anything more because so much is happening for them through the sound that it would overwhelm them to have to consider other realities.

But the sensorium of the Nigerian priest and the African liturgists has taught them to focus their material energies in a different pattern, one characterized by a kinetic use of the body and a sonic idiom that stresses rhythmic rather than harmonic complexities.

One is not "better" than the other; one is not in any absolute sense "more meaningful" than the other. Each creates meaning by providing a choreography of material elements that people raised in their particular culture can connect in patterns that illumine their existence as individuals and as community. When people say of a sermon or service that it was "meaningful," they are indicating that the preacher or worship leaders so organized the use of eye, ear, body, and language that it was congruent with their sensorium while providing enough novelty that it admitted new light or a sense of the Spirit or a receiving of the word of God or whatever other way they have of expressing delight at the illumination of their world.

This does not mean that we human beings are incapable of widening our cultural repertoire. As we saw in earlier chapters, people do have a God-given capacity to learn new visual, oral, somatic, and linguistic idioms. Sometimes it happens with relative ease, as when we hear a new kind of music that steals our heart. But often it takes a great deal of work, and sometimes it proves impossible.

The Theological Implication of Cultural Analysis

Over these last twenty-five years I have worked with more and more religious groups struggling with how to embrace multiculturalism while remaining faithful to their historic identities. I have now abandoned my hope that there is some principle or method that would make it possible to bring a full and satisfying integration of all our highly variegated sensoria. Instead, I have come to see that our hope for mutual understanding lies in two complemental directions.

The first direction is what I have proposed throughout this book: self-conscious attention to the cultural sensorium that has shaped us and others so that we, at the very least, have an appreciation for why there are such great differences between us.

The second direction is theological. Analyzing the deep, material roots of our cultural differences leads us to realize that the only one capable of understanding all sensoria simultaneously is God. When God's spirit is present among us, then we are gifted with a glimpse of the divine vision, a moment of Pentecost that recapitulates the first Pentecost (Acts 2:5–12). People of multiple languages do not suddenly speak one language, but a universal understanding is granted to them while they each speak in their distinct tongue. The result is amazement and astonishment.

I believe it honors the spirit of Luke's account of Pentecost to expand the meaning of "language" to include the visual, oral, and somatic idioms of the different groups. Pentecost happens when the Spirit of God intersects our varied sensoria and opens our hearts to acknowledge that the grace and wonder of God are manifest through multiple idioms. Pentecost is no longer the reversal of the story of Babel: People still speak their own varied tongues. Instead, Pentecost reveals that our unity does not depend on melting away our differences. Our unity is found in the living Spirit who created us all and who can use our varied idioms to express divine grace, love, and justice. We undertake an analysis of the interrelationship of culture, worship, and preaching, not simply to work out the practicalities of understanding one another, as important as that is. Rather, we carry on this work because through it we may be awakened anew to the astounding work of the Spirit, and thereby be empowered to give all of us to all of God.

NOTES

Chapter 1: Culture as a Constellation of the Senses

[1]John McDargh, *Psychoanalytic Object Relations Theory and the Study of Religion: On Faith and the Imaging of God* (Lanham, Md.: University Press of America, 1983), 215, quoted in Carroll Saussy, *God Images and Self Esteem: Empowering Women in a Patriarchal Society* (Louisville: Westminster/John Knox Press, 1991), 29.

[2]Eunjoo Mary Kim, *Preaching the Presence of God: A Homiletic from an Asian American Perspective* (Valley Forge, Pa.: Judson Press, 1999), 109.

[3]Professor Linda Thomas.

[4]Edward B. Tylor, *Primitive Culture: Researches into the Development of Mythology, Philosophy, Religion, Art, and Custom* (London: John Murray, 1871), 1.

[5]Franz Boas, quoted in Elvin Hatch, *Culture and Morality: The Relativity of Values in Anthropology* (New York: Columbia University Press, 1983), 52–53.

[6]Sheila Greeve Davaney, "Theology and the Turn to Cultural Analysis," in *Converging on Culture: Theologians in Dialogue with Cultural Analysis and Criticism,* ed. Delwin Brown, Sheila Greeve Davaney, Kathryn Tanner (New York: Oxford University Press, 2001), 5.

[7]Eugene A. Nida, *Customs and Cultures: Anthropology for Christian Missions* (New York: Harper & Brothers, 1954), 28.

[8]Walter J. Ong, S. J., *The Presence of the Word: Some Prolegomena for Cultural and Religious History* (New Haven, Conn.: Yale University Press, 1967), 6.

[9]John Bowker, ed., *The Oxford Dictionary of World Religions* (New York: Oxford University Press, 1997), 819.

[10]Stephen Buckland, "Ritual, Bodies and 'Cultural Memory,'" in *Liturgy and the Body,* ed. Louis-Marie Chauvet and François Kabasele Lumbala (London: Concilium SCM Press, 1995), 52.

[11]*The Oxford English Dictionary* (Oxford: Oxford University Press, 1989), 121.

[12]Nathan Mitchell, "Emerging Rituals in Contemporary Culture," in Chauvet and Lumbala, *Liturgy and the Body,* 121. Mitchell is paraphrasing Erik Erikson in "Ontogeny of Ritualization in Man," *Philosophical Transactions of the Royal Society of London* 251 (Series B, 1966): 337–49.

[13]Kathy Black, *Worship Across Cultures: A Handbook* (Nashville: Abingdon Press, 1998), 11.

[14]Paul F. Bradshaw, *The Search for the Origins of Christian Worship: Sources and Methods for the Study of Early Liturgy* (New York: Oxford University Press, 1992), 68.

[15]Othmar Keel, *The Symbolism of the Biblical World: Ancient Near Eastern Iconography and the Book of Psalms,* trans. Timothy J. Hallett (New York: Seabury Press, 1978), 7.

[16]J. Wendell Mapson, Jr., *The Ministry of Music in the Black Church* (Valley Forge, Pa.: Judson Press, 1984), 32, as quoted in Brenda Eatman Aghahowa, *Praising in Black and White: Unity and Diversity in Christian Worship* (Cleveland: United Church Press, 1996), 19.

[17]Ronald J. Allen, Barbara Shires Blaisdell, Scott Black Johnston, *Theology for Preaching: Authority, Truth and Knowledge of God in a Postmodern Ethos* (Nashville: Abingdon Press, 1997), 119–20.

[18]Hatch, 53, quoting Clyde Kluckhohn, *Mirror for Man* (New York and Toronto: McGraw-Hill, 1949), 26.

[19]Sigmund Freud, "One of the Difficulties of Psychoanalysis," in *Freud: Character and Culture: Psychoanalysis Applied to Anthropology, Mythology, Folklore, Literature, and Culture in General,* ed. Philip Rieff (New York: Collier Books, 1963), 185–87.

[20]Neil Postman, *Technopoly: The Surrender of Culture to Technology* (New York: Vintage Books, 1993).

[21]Ibid., 90.

[22]Ong, 6.

[23]Davaney, 8. Davaney is referring to Lawrence E. Sullivan, "Seeking an End to the Primary Text or 'Putting an End to the Text as Primary,'" in *Beyond the Classics? Essays in Religious Studies and Liberal Education,* ed. Frank E. Reynolds and Sheryl L. Buckhalter (Atlanta: Scholars Press, 1990), 42.

[24]Tex Sample, *The Spectacle of Worship in a Wired World* (Nashville: Abingdon Press, 1998), 16.

[25]Margaret R. Miles, *Image as Insight: Visual Understanding in Western Christianity and Secular Culture* (Boston: Beacon Press, 1985), 20.

[26]Jyoti Sahi, "The Body in Search of Interiority" in Chauvet and Lumbala, 88–89.

[27]*The Oxford Dictionary of World Religions,* 819–20.

[28]Leonora Tubbs Tisdale, *Preaching as Local Theology and Folk Art* (Minneapolis: Fortress Press, 1997), 15.

[29]Wayne A. Meeks, ed., *The HarperCollins Study Bible* (New York: HarperCollins, 1993), 279.

[30]Henry George Liddell and Robert Scott, *An Intermediate Greek-English Lexicon* (Oxford: Oxford University Press, 1961), 385.

[31]Professor James B. Ashbrook, now deceased, who taught pastoral care at Colgate Rochester Divinity School and then at Garrett Evangelical Theological Seminary.

[32]Saussy, 39.

[33]Sahi, 89.

[34]William F. Arndt and F. Wilbur Gingrich, *A Greek-English Lexicon of the New Testament and Other Early Christian Literature* (Chicago: University of Chicago Press, 1957), 569.

[35]Davaney, 4.

[36]Tisdale, 56–57. See especially her chapter on "Exegeting the Congregation" for a clear summary of ways preachers can be participant-observers of the churches they come to serve.

[37]Robert J. Schreiter, *Constructing Local Theologies* (Maryknoll, N.Y.: Orbis Books, 1985), 29.

[38]William James, *The Varieties of Religious Experience,* as quoted in Robin Knowles Wallace, *Moving Toward Emancipatory Language: A Study of Recent Hymns* (Lanham, Md.: Scarecrow Press, 1999), 78.

[39]Kathy Black, *A Healing Homiletic: Preaching and Disability* (Nashville: Abingdon Press, 1996), 13.

Chapter 2: Eye

[1]Clara H. Scott wrote the hymn in 1895. It is still found in many Protestant hymnals.

[2]Tex Sample, *The Spectacle of Worship in a Wired World* (Nashville: Abingdon Press, 1998), 16.

[3]Paul Corby Finney, *The Invisible God: The Earliest Christians on Art* (New York: Oxford University Press, 1994), 7.

[4]Bob Scribner, "The Image and the Reformation," in *Disciplines of Faith: Studies in Religion, Politics and Patriarchy,* ed. Jim Obelkevich, Lyndal Roper, and Raphael Samuel (London: Routledge and Kegan Paul, 1987), 542.

[5] Margaret R. Miles, *Image as Insight: Visual Understanding in Western Christianity and Secular Culture* (Boston: Beacon Press, 1985), 99.

[6] Scribner, 546.

[7] Quoted by George D. S. Henderson, "Narrative Illustration and Theological Exposition in Medieval Art," in *Religion and Humanism: Papers Read at the Eighteenth Summer Meeting and the Nineteenth Winter Meeting of the Ecclesiastical History Society,* ed. Keith Robbins, vol. 17 of *Studies in Church History* (Oxford: Published for the Ecclesiastical History Society by Basil Blackwell, 1981), 19.

[8] Averil Cameron, "The Language of Images: The Rise of Icons and Christian Representation," in *The Church and the Arts,* ed. Diana Wood (Oxford: Blackwell Publishers, 1992), 2.

[9] Finney, 4.

[10] G. I. T. Machin, "British Churches and the Cinema," in Wood, *Church and the Arts,* 480.

[11] Ibid.

[12] Finney, 42. The word's are Finney's summation of Octavius's argument.

[13] Ibid., 43.

[14] Thomas F. Mathews [sic], *The Clash of Gods: A Reinterpretation of Early Christian Art* (Princeton: Princeton University Press, 1993), 11.

[15] Cameron, 19.

[16] Ibid., 41.

[17] Mary Gordon, "The Gospel According to Saint Mark: Parts of a Journal," in *Incarnation: Contemporary Writers on the New Testament,* ed. Alfred Corn (New York: Penguin Books, 1990), 12–13.

[18] Miles, 99. See earlier in this chapter for a discussion of the imbalance in the late medieval church.

[19] Sample, 29.

[20] Miles, 99.

[21] Lynn M. Haims, "Puritan Iconography: The Art of Edward Taylor's *God's Determinations,*" in *Puritan Poets and Poetics: Seventeenth-Century American Poetry in Theory and Practice,* ed. Peter White (University Park: Pennsylvania State University Press, 1985), 84.

[22] Ibid., 88.

[23] Ibid., 84.

[24] Ibid.

[25] Finney, 108.

[26] Ibid., 152.

[27] Ibid., 229.

[28] James A. Francis, "The Quest of the Ahistorical Jesus: Image, Text, and the Christianization of the Roman Empire," unpublished paper, 14–15.

[29] Clement of Alexandria, *The Teacher(Logo Paidagogos),* written around 200 C.E., as quoted in Finney, 111.

[30] Mathews, 4–5.

[31] Ibid., 141.

[32] Francis, 11.

[33] Mathews, 180.

Chapter 3: Ear

[1] Richard F. Ward, *Speaking of the Holy: The Art of Communication in Preaching* (St. Louis: Chalice Press, 2001), 53.

[2] Edmund A. Steimle, Morris J. Niedenthal, Charles L. Rice, *Preaching the Story* (Philadelphia: Fortress Press, 1980), 11.

[3] Evans E. Crawford, *The Hum: Call and Response in African American Preaching* (Nashville: Abingdon Press, 1995), 16.

[4]Gerald L. Davis, *I Got the Word in Me and I Can Sing It, You Know: A Study of the Performed African-American Sermon* (Philadelphia: University of Pennsylvania Press, 1985), 9.

[5]Ibid., 17.

[6]Lee McGee, *Wrestling with the Patriarchs: Retrieving Women's Voices in Preaching* (Nashville: Abingdon Press, 1996), 19.

[7]Jane E. Vennard, *Be Still: Designing and Leading Contemplative Retreats* (Bethesda, Md.: Alban Institute, 2000), 14–15.

[8]Eunjoo Mary Kim, *Preaching the Presence of God: A Homiletic from an Asian American Perspective* (Valley Forge, Pa.: Judson Press, 1999), 110.

[9]Crawford, 17.

[10]Kim, 111.

[11]Vennard, 15.

[12]Mary Donovan Turner and Mary Lin Hudson, *Saved from Silence: Finding Women's Voice in Preaching* (St. Louis: Chalice Press, 1999), 15. I am especially indebted to this book for my discussion of silence and voice.

[13]Barbara Brown Taylor, *When God Is Silent* (Boston: Cowley Publications, 1998), 51.

[14]Nelle Morton, *The Journey Is Home* (Boston: Beacon Press, 1985), 87, as quoted in Turner and Hudson, *Saved from Silence*, 6.

[15]Henry Wilson Steward, *The Speaking God: Luther's Theology of Preaching* (Ann Arbor, Mich.: University Microfilms International, 1977), 121, as quoted in Kathy Black, *A Healing Homiletic*, 99. See Black's book for a helpful discussion of the negative ways a theology of hearing can impact deaf culture.

[16]Lawrance Thompson and R. H. Winnick, *Robert Frost: A Biography* (New York: Hold, Rinehart and Winston, 1981), 210–11.

[17]Brian Wren, *Praying Twice: The Music and Words of Congregational Song* (Louisville: Westminster John Knox Press, 2000), 49.

[18]I am indebted to a church musician and colleague named John Repulski, who made this observation in a class we teach about ritual and worship.

[19]Leonard Meyer, *Meaning and Emotion in Music* (Chicago: Chicago University Press, 1956), 62, as quoted in Wren, 57.

[20]Thomas H. Troeger, *Borrowed Light: Hymn Texts, Prayers, and Poems* (New York: Oxford University Press, 1994), 144.

[21]Wren, 161–62.

[22]Quentin Faulkner, *Wiser than Despair: The Evolution of Ideas in the Relationship of Music and the Christian Church* (Westport, Conn.: Greenwood Press, 1996), 47. I am drawing heavily from Faulkner's book in the discussion that follows.

[23]Quoted in the Introduction to James McKinnon, *Music in Early Christian Literature* (New York: Cambridge University Press, 1989), 4–5. McKinnon provides a wide selection of primary source material on the church's understanding of music up through Augustine.

[24]McKinnon, 46.

[25]Clement of Alexandria in McKinnon, 30.

[26]See Faulkner. The book documents not only the history of how these Greek canons were adapted by the church but also how they continued to be invoked over many centuries of Christian worship history.

[27]McKinnon, 34.

[28]Ibid., 2.

[29]Faulkner, 159.

[30]Marion J. Hatchett, *Commentary on the American Prayer Book* (San Francisco: HarperSanFrancisco, 1995), 117.

[31]I have taken the idea of comparing the two from Faulkner, 164.

[32]See *Chalice Hymnal* (St. Louis: Chalice Press, 1995), no. 33.

[33]*The Book of Common Prayer* (New York: Church Hymnal Corporation, 1979), 95–96.

[34]Faulkner, 190.

[35]Joseph Gelineau, S.J., *Voices and Instruments in Christian Worship,* trans. Clifford Howell, S.J. (London: Burns Y Oates, 1964), 44, as quoted in Faulkner, 9.

[36]McKinnon, 155.

[37]Ibid., 22.

[38]For a full account of the process with many fascinating quotations from ancient sources, see Faulkner, chapters 2, 3, and 4.

[39]Romanticism is a notoriously slippery term, but once we allow for the inadequacy of any definition we can say that it is "used to describe literature, written mainly in the 2 decades 1830-1850, and applied to music written in the period c. 1830 to c. 1900…[E]motional and picturesque expression appeared to be more important than formal or structural considerations," Michael Kennedy, *The Oxford Dictionary of Music* (New York: Oxford University Press, 1985), 603.

[40]See Faulkner for an exhaustive treatment of this history with thorough documentation from original sources.

[41]Faulkner, 203.

[42]Thomas H. Troeger, "For God Risk Everything," copyright 1996, Oxford University Press. The text is published with a beautiful new musical setting in Sally Ann Morris, *Giving Thanks in Song and Prayer: Hymntunes of Sally Ann Morris for Congregation, Choir, and Accompaniment* (Chicago: GIA Publications, 1998), 12–13.

[43]W. A. Mathieu, *The Listening Book: Discovering Your Own Music* (Boston & London: Shambhala, 1991), 129.

[44]Paul Westermeyer, *Te Deum: The Church and Music* (Minneapolis: Fortress Press, 1998), 319.

[45]Sigvald Tveit, "Hymnody and Identity," *The Hymn: A Journal of Congregational Song* 51, no. 4 (October 2000): 10.

[46]Ibid.

Chapter 4: Body

[1]Stephen Buckland, "Ritual, Bodies and 'Cultural Memory,'" in *Liturgy and the Body*, ed. Louis-Marie Chauvet and François Kabasele Lumbala (London: Concilium SCM Press, 1995), 50.

[2]Ibid., 52.

[3]Thomas Hardy, *The Mayor of Casterbridge* (1886; reprint, Boston: Houghton Mifflin, 1962), 52.

[4]Jyoti Sahi, "The Body in Search of Interiority," in Chauvet and Lumbala, 88.

[5]Nathan Mitchell, "Emerging Rituals in Contemporary Culture," in Chauvet and Lumbala, 121.

[6]Buckland, 51.

[7]Othmar Keel, *The Symbolism of the Biblical World: Ancient Near Eastern Iconography and the Book of Psalms,* trans. Timothy J. Hallett (New York: Seabury Press, 1978).

[8]Ibid., 319, fig. 428.

[9]Ibid., 354, fig. 479.

[10]Paul Corby Finney, *The Invisible God: The Earliest Christians on Art* (New York: Oxford University Press, 1994), 40.

[11]Quoted in Finney, 105.

[12]Elochukwu E. Uzukwu, "Body and Memory in African Liturgy," in Chauvet and Lumbala, 73.

[13]Arnobius, in McKinnon, 49.

[14]Chrysostom, in McKinnon, 84.

[15]Teresa Berger, "Women as Alien Bodies in the Body of Christ? The Place of Women in Worship," in Chauvet and Lumbala, 113.

[16]Ibid., 115.

[17]Thomas F. Mathews, [sic], *The Clash of Gods: A Reinterpretation of Early Christian Art* (Princeton: Princeton University Press, 1993), 140.

[18]Margaret R. Miles, *Image as Insight: Visual Understanding in Western Christianity and Secular Culture* (Boston: Beacon Press, 1985), 19.

[19]Ibid., 27.

[20]Ibid., 56.

[21]Mathews, 121 and 123. The text is continuous; page 122 features artistic images of Christ.

[22]Uzukwu, 73.

[23]Miles, 42.

[24]Moshe Barasch, "How the Hidden Becomes Visible," in *Secrecy and Concealment: Studies in the History of Mediterranean and Near Eastern Religions,* ed. Hans G. Kippenberg and Guy G. Stroumsa (New York: E. J. Brill, 1995), 389–90.

[25]Francis Jacques, "From Language Games to 'Textual Games,'" in Chauvet and Lumbala, 10.

[26]Barasch, 388.

[27]Mathews, 114.

[28]Keel, 315–16.

[29]Christopher B. Turner, "Revivalism and Welsh Society in the 19th Century," in *Disciplines of Faith: Studies in Religion, Politics and Patriarchy,* ed. Jim Obelkevich, Lyndal Roper, and Raphael Samuel (London: Routledge and Kegan Paul, 1987), 312.

[30]Brenda Eatman Aghahowa, *Praising in Black and White: Unity and Diversity in Christian Worship* (Cleveland: United Church Press, 1996), 8.

[31]Ibid., 72.

[32]Ibid., 28.

[33]Uzukwu, 73.

[34]Ibid.

Chapter 5: Language

[1]Sheila Greeve Davaney, "Theology and the Turn to Cultural Analysis," in *Converging on Culture: Theologians in Dialogue with Cultural Analysis and Criticism,* ed. Delwin Brown, Sheila Greeve Davaney, Kathryn Tanner (New York: Oxford University Press, 2001), 9.

[2]Leonora Tubbs Tisdale, *Preaching as Local Theology and Folk Art* (Minneapolis: Fortress Press, 1997), 1–7.

[3]Michael Edwards, *Towards a Christian Poetics* (Grand Rapids, Mich.: Eerdmans, 1984), 137.

[4]Wendell Berry, *Standing by Words* (San Francisco: North Point Press, 1983), 207.

[5]Michel Foucault, as quoted in Ada Maria Isasi-Diaz, "Creating a Liberating Culture: Latinas' Subversive Narratives," in *Converging on Culture: Theologians in Dialogue with Cultural Analysis and Criticism,* ed. Delwin Brown, Sheila Greeve Davaney, Kathryn Tanner (New York: Oxford University Press, 2001), 130.

[6]Teresa L. Fry Brown, *God Don't Like Ugly: African American Women Handing on Spiritual Values* (Nashville: Abingdon Press, 2000), 65.

[7]Nelle Morton, as quoted in Mary Donovan Turner and Mary Lin Hudson, *Saved from Silence: Finding Women's Voice in Preaching* (St. Louis: Chalice Press, 1999), 6. The passage originally appears in Morton, *The Journey Is Home* (Boston: Beacon Press, 1985), 87.

[8]Among the works that I am drawing from in this discussion are: James A. Sanders, "Contextual Hermeneutics," in Richard Lischer, *Theories of Preaching: Selected Readings in the Homiletical Tradition* (Durham, N.C.: Labyrinth Press, 1987), 190; David E. Aune, *The New Testament in Its Literary Environment* (Philadelphia: Westminster Press, 1987); Peter J. Gomes, *The Good Book: Reading the Bible with Mind and Heart* (New York: William Morrow, 1996).

[9]Acts 11:26; 26:28; 1 Peter 4:16.

[10]John P. Meier, "Antioch," in Paul J. Achtemeier, *Harper's Bible Dictionary* (San Francisco: HarperSan Francisco, 1985), 33.

[11]D. S. Wallace-Hadrill, *Christian Antioch: A Study of Early Christian Thought in the East* (Cambridge: Cambridge University Press, 1982), 14–15.

[12]Othmar Keel, *The Symbolism of the Biblical World: Ancient Near Eastern Iconography and the Book of Psalms,* trans. Timothy J. Hallett (New York: Seabury Press, 1978), 355.

[13]Raymond E. Brown, *An Introduction to the New Testament* (New York: Doubleday, 1997), 605.

[14]"Probably in 1:15–20 an extant hymn has been adapted," Ibid., 600.

[15]F. W. Beare, *A Commentary on the Epistle to the Philippians,* 3d ed. (London: Adam & Charles Black, 1976), 148.

[16]Fred B. Craddock, *Philippians,* Interpretation: A Bible Commentary for Teaching and Preaching (Atlanta: John Knox Press, 1985), 73.

[17]Article 76, various Web sites.

[18]Henry Van Dyke, *Companionable Books* (New York: Charles Scribner's Sons, 1923), 10.

[19]Sallie McFague, *Metaphorical Theology: Models of God in Religious Language* (Minneapolis: Fortress Press), 28.

[20]Gomes, 6.

[21]Ibid., 13.

[22]Ronald J. Allen, *Interpreting the Gospel: An Introduction to Preaching* (St. Louis: Chalice Press, 1998), 62.

[23]Gomes, 40.

[24]James A. Sanders, "Contextual Hermeneutics," in Lischer, *Theories of Preaching,* 190.

[25]Van Dyke, vii.

[26]Ibid., 3–4.

[27]Ibid., 5.

[28]Nathan A. Scott, Jr., *The Poetics of Belief: Studies in Coleridge, Arnold, Pater, Santayan, Stevens, and Heidegger* (Chapel Hill: University of North Carolina Press, 1985), 13–14. The quote within the quote is from Wallace Stevens, "Notes Toward a Supreme Fiction."

Chapter 6: Meaning

[1]Elochukwu Uzukwu, "Body and Memory in African Liturgy," in *Liturgy and the Body*, ed. Louis-Marie Chauvet and François Kabasale Lumbala (London: Concilium SCM Press, 1995), 74.

[2]Ibid.

INDEX

A
Augustine, 62

B
Bible
  as book, library, tree, 118
  different rhetorical cultures,
    107–11, 119–20
  expanding our metaphors
    for, 113–16
  ontology, 116–18
  use of for and against
    images, 30–33
body
  female body, ambivalence
    about in Christian
    worship, 84–88
  somatic idiom, 73–78, 88–97
  suspicion of in early
    Christian worship, 81
  tensions about in the history
    of Christian worship,
    83–84
  use of in the Bible, 79

C
Calvin, 28
Christian, history of the word,
  104–5
Clement of Alexandria, 37, 54
Copernicus, 12–13
culture
  analysis, 22–23
  contradictions and complex-
    ities of church culture,
    35–36
  definitions, 3–5

  humility and pride in our
    own culture, 69–70
  implicit questions a culture
    asks and answers, 5
  lack of awareness of our
    own culture, 3
  mastery of a somatic idiom,
    73–75 (*see also* ritualization)
  rhetorical cultures, 101–2,
    105–7
  rhetorical cultures and
    theology, 111– 13
  sonic culture, 52–53
  tensions between cultures,
    11–12
  theological implication of
    cultural analysis, 124–25

D
Darwin, 12–13

E
ear (*see* sound)
Erasmus, 29
eye (*see* images *and* visual
  theology)

F
Freud, 12–13

G
Greco–Roman art
  impact on church, 36–38
grid for cultural analysis, 14–18

H
"How Great Thou Art," 55–56

I
iconoclasm, 26–27
images
as access to the divine, 31–33
hunger for images, 34–35
on page or in church, 27–29
power of images, 33–34

J
Japan noodle parable, 1–3

L
language
limits to language, 99–100
Luther, Martin, 27–28

M
meaning
as a construction of the sensorium, 121–22
music
different meanings awakened, 50–51
fragmentation of church's theology of music, 63–64
prayer for the ministries of music, 70–71
principles for understanding function of music in church, 60–69
singing and creaturehood, 65–66
singing and salvation, 66–68
spectrum of church music, 68–69

P
Paul the Apostle, 9–11
pluralism
historic reality in the church, 8–11 (*see also* culture)

preaching
post–Christian challenge, 103–4
practical questions in light of cultural changes, 95–97
rhetorical balancing act, 102–3
sound of sermon and its impact, 45–46
Puritans, 35
Pythagoras, 53

R
ritualization, 6–8

S
Sample, Tex, 34
sensorium, 4–6, 17–18, 24, 29–30, 122–23
Shema, 21–22
silence, 46–48
somatic idiom (*see* body *and* culture)
sound
ability to override the verbal, 57
associative patterns, 43–44
historic transformation of church's sonic culture, 55–57
music (*see* music)
sense (meaning) conveyed by sound, 49–50
in sermons, 45–46
sonic culture exercises for a congregation, 58–60
sound and silence: varied functions, 48–49

T
Taylor, Edward, 34
Te Deum, 55–57

Trullo, Council in, 29

V
visual theology
    practical exercises for
        church, 40
    thinking through images,
        38–39

W
worship (*see* body, culture,
    images, music)